Vintage Edwardian Murder

by the same author

'R.A.B.' Study of a Statesman
Hussein of Jordan
Gordon, Mandarin and Pasha
Golden Orchid
Opium Venture
Java Weed
Women Who Murder
Vintage Victorian Murder

Vintage Edwardian Murder

GERALD SPARROW

ARTHUR BARKER LIMITED
5 Winsley Street London W1

SBN 0 213 00396 1
Printed in Great Britain by Bristol Typesetting Co. Ltd.
Barton Manor, St Philips, Bristol

Contents

Contents

I

Those Were the Days

Albert Edward, King of the United Kingdom of Great Britain and Ireland and of the British Dominions beyond the Seas, Defender of the Faith, Emperor of India, came to the throne on 22 January 1901, his mother, Queen Victoria, having died that evening surrounded by her children and grandchildren at Osborne.

The old Queen had reigned for sixty-three years, seven months and two days. The nation had become accustomed to regarding her as the symbol of Britain and her vast Empire that included more than a quarter of the world. They could hardly believe that, at last, she was gone.

The Prince was in his sixtieth year when he became king and his mother had kept all the reins of power in her own hands, delegating very little to her son whom, to the last, she insisted in regarding as amiable, even lovable, but not very mature.

Not permitted to play any political role, the Prince had devoted himself, throughout his life, to travel, pleasure and such ceremonial duties as he was allowed to undertake. He had married Alexandra, a captivating Danish princess. He had suffered one serious illness that rallied public opinion to his support.

As he was naturally pleasure-loving, and had the means to indulge himself, it was inevitable that King Edward, when he became king, should pursue, with suitable discretion, the way of life he loved. He loved beautiful women, so he had beautiful mistresses; he loved racing, so he supported the turf. He loved champagne and great and gay house parties, so he graced the great houses of England where his visit, with his own flag flying over the house, was long prepared for, and a dazzling occasion.

He was very Germanic, speaking English with a German intonation and, in later years, he lost his grace and became unwieldy. But he was instantly recognizable. His Tyrolean hat, his cigar, his cloak, his whole air of rich and benevolent autocracy made it impossible not to know that this was the King. There was no one like him. Although he looked Germanic he was in a number of ways also very English. His hobbies were horse racing, yachting, shooting.

Although throughout the year he lived at each of his homes, Buckingham Palace, St James's Palace, Balmoral and Sandringham, he was happiest either as Squire of Sandringham or as a guest at the house of one of his friends where the other guests could be carefully and privately chosen, so that the King should never be bored. When this disaster threatened he had a disconcerting habit of drumming on the card table with his fingers – the signal for a lady in favour to glide up and be seated by his side.

He loved France, but was suspicious of Germany, and he was jealous and resentful of his nephew, the pushing young Emperor Wilhelm. When this young man turned up at Cowes, his yacht escorted by six German warships, Prince Edward had fumed at 'this shocking ostentation and bad taste'. Edward was a little garish and grand himself but he did not like explosions of grandeur in others.

Very slowly the British public realized that the great Queen had, after all, been mortal and was no more. And they took to King Edward. He was a human kind of man. If he loved gambling and drink and women, why they loved gambling and drink and women too. He might be a German prince but he had become very much an English king. They did not mind his dedication to pleasure. They thought it very natural. They liked the rich, rare whiff of the man and the image that grew of him, racing at Ascot, shooting at Sandringham, or sailing at Cowes. As for politics, the King knew the rules, and his reactions on the whole were the reactions of his people. He reflected with astonishing fidelity, as his mother had done, what the man in the street thought, but could not always express.

His reign was the last comparatively untroubled one of the golden era of British monarchy. It was the last decade during which the great landowners still ruled the English roost. Chatsworth, Welbeck, Dunrobin, Arundel, these houses were centres of power as well as of prestige. Society meant the small, favoured few who were received at Court and were the King's friends or belonged to the great families. King Edward extended the boundaries but only very slightly, admitting a few very rich Jews who, up to then, had been excluded from English social life at the top, with the exception of figures to whom no rules applied, like Lord Beaconsfield, formerly Disraeli.

The sun shone everywhere on the British flag. One could take a ship in London or Southampton and sail to Hong Kong, never calling at a port where the Union Jack did not fly. The certainties of the Victorian age continued to flourish. The people believed that British rule brought untold blessings to the natives, especially to the black races of India and Africa; that British naval superiority was an absolute essential for world peace; that it was natural for the world to come to London to seek imperial favour; and that the division of the public into three great classes – the ruling class, the middle class and the working class – was a fact of life and added stability to the national structure of a mighty imperial power.

They believed that you had to work to live, that the State owed you nothing, that respect for authority was essential, that traitors and murderers should be hanged by the neck until they were dead. They believed in their King, in the House of Lords, in the Commons and they believed in their judges, saying that the whole world envied (among other things) the British judicial system, the British jury system and the rule of law as it obtained and was enforced in England.

The political leaders attempted to reflect these attitudes in their orations and no one did this more cleverly than Disraeli had done under the old Queen.

The Tory Party, unless it is a national Party, is nothing. It is not a confederacy of nobles, it is not a democratic multitude. It is a party formed from all the numerous classes of the realm – classes alike and equal before the law, but whose different conditions and different aims add vigour and variety to our national life.

Now under the gay and dashing King Edward this was still the national philosophy. But the first permissive society had been born. The old Queen's implacable puritanism was dead. England was going to enjoy herself – and she did.

Against this background some of the most extraordinary murder cases in the long catalogue of crime were enacted in the courts. Some of them, like the King himself, seemed larger than life. The popular British press had just been born and the great trials were reported verbatim.

Into this period, too, strode the greatest advocates, men who would have dominated their fellows in any walk of life, while the judges really had to be seen to be believed. Sometimes they seemed to be avenging angels determined that the prisoner should not escape and that society should exact its vengeance. But the Edwardian juries were steady, unexpectedly independent, shrewd and fair.

It was a great and a glamorous period in the courts and it is to the Old Bailey that we now go to watch those men accused of the dreadful crime of murder, facing death if the jury found them guilty, but returning to freedom if the verdict was not guilty. On these words their life depended.

The odd thing about all this was that the nation appeared to be very much more united, very much more ' one people ' than it does today when bitter industrial disputes disfigure our public life. The Edwardians had no race problems, few public money problems, no religious problems. They believed in racialism. They were quite sure (as the South Africans are today) that the white men were in every way superior to the black men. Money presented no difficulty. It was never spoken of in polite society, the assumption being that everyone had it. Religion was, as they say, no problem. The Church of England and the squirearchy dominated the country. The parson and the squire ruled the village. People went to church because it was regarded as bad form, and as setting a bad example, not to be seen to go to church on Sunday.

Hypocrites? Were they all hypocrites? I do not think they were anything like as hypocritical as the poor deluded fools who whine for Mao Tse-Tung or Lenin, the arch-priests of tyranny. The Edwardian hypocrisies were petty in comparison. Yes, men had mistresses, but they were not allowed to intrude, and they were not known as 'girl friends'. Nor were adult women over twenty-one referred to as 'girls'. The whole distorted nomenclature which we employ today had not yet been born.

They did not pretend that all men were equal for they knew very well that they were not, and they suspected that a dead and frozen equality could be obtained only by keeping down the few so that the many could catch up.

The Edwardians were down to earth. They were worldly, yes, often they were wily, but they pretended only in order to make life more pleasing, more fun, and more livable.

But was it fun for the working man? He could be sacked at a moment's notice. His wages were low. He had to treat his superiors with respect. He had to obey. He had to do all these things, yet often he contrived to enjoy himself in the gusty, gay life of the time. With gin at fourpence a glass, and good books at eighteen pence each, he could gratify his appetite or his mind, while the girls, for all their long skirts and big hats, managed to keep the men occupied. It was a rumbustious age in which everyone felt that it was good to be alive.

Life is not made by money. It is the tragedy of the modern Trade Union Movement that it has sunk to the position of being dedicated solely to attempting to squeeze more money out of 'management'. The Edwardians, of course, were still talking about masters and men with no sense of shame.

The Edwardians believed in their land of hope and glory, because life in many ways was glorious and certainly full of hope. To be born an Englishman, that was the greatest good fortune, and even to be born Scots, Welsh or Irish was not too bad. At least, and thank God, one was not a foreigner. Foreigners did not include Americans. They were in a special category – members of the family who had emigrated.

King Edward died on 6 May 1910, but the Edwardian age really ended on 4 August 1914. The world changed for good that day. The glittering world of English feudalism was never to be seen again. So the cases in this book are taken from the years 1901 to 1914, when the great Empire went to war.

2

The Camden Town Murder

Of all the instruments of murder, the knife is the most dramatic and the most dreadful. Where poison is used it is the poison itself that kills the victim – the murderer merely administers it. Where a gun is made the instrument of death, although the murderer may pull the trigger, there is a mechanical result, an explosion, followed by the ejection of the bullet fired towards the body of the victim. So that in the case both of murder by poison and murder by shooting the murderer is not so directly and physically involved as the man who uses a knife to butcher his victim.

Even when a knife is used there are degrees of horror. In England to be stabbed in the back is so evocative of treachery that it has become a phrase in the language. To be stabbed through the heart has its own dramatic connotation, but when we get a woman lying on a bed who has had her throat cut from ear to ear so that her arteries are severed and the sheets and pillows are drenched with the great gush of her blood, then we know we are dealing with murder so vile or so mad that it takes all our human understanding to appreciate how so dreadful an act could, in fact have been perpetrated.

In the year 1906 the Midland Railway employed a young man named Bertram Shaw as a cook or chef on their excellent trains that ran to the north of England. There are those still alive who can remember these trains. They were spotless. They ran on time. To be even a few minutes late was regarded by the company as a shameful thing, and they served very good food and wine with a dedication based on the fact that they had to please their customers in order to make a profit.

Now most of the passengers on the Midland Railway during the day, when they wanted luncheon, would put their heads out of the carriage window at Rugby or at Crewe and call a boy who would immediately bring them a luncheon basket which usually contained half a cold chicken, half a bottle of white wine, some hot rolls, butter and a variety of cheese. It was only in the evening and during the night that cooks were needed on the train to serve the passengers with more elaborate meals. Bertram Shaw was glad to have his job. He earned nearly £5 per week and there was a sense of excitement about it. The great steam locomotives would roar through the night and the passengers often included the famous and sometimes the infamous. From the cook's galley Bertram, decked out in spotless white, with his chef's hat perched firmly on his head, could see quite a lot and the cooks took a share in the tips that the waiters collected. As he was a young man and, technically at least, unmarried, he did not mind the night work. You cannot have everything and the railway company were good, if strict, employers. He usually got back to London in the early morning and made his way to the small flat he occupied at 29 St Paul's Road, Camden Town. Some months before this he had taken a prostitute whose real name was Emily Dimmock – although she was always known as Phyllis – off the streets and into his home. The couple were then known as Mr and Mrs Bertram Shaw.

Bertram was used to returning in the morning to be greeted by Phyllis, who was a lively person and who it seemed loved him, partly perhaps because he was an attractive young man and partly because of the incredible thing he had done, sweeping aside all prejudice and seeking to marry her, for that was his intention. He was planning to introduce Phyllis to his family and so pave the way towards marriage and children. He thought he could win his father over without too much difficulty, but he expected his mother to put up some resistance for she had been brought up as a Methodist and 'scarlet women' was a phrase she had used from time to time, warning her son to avoid such people, who were the spawn of the Devil.

Bertram turned the handle of the door but could not get

in. He thought it was jammed so he knocked and pushed it. There was no reply, which was odd unless Phyllis was already out, which was unlikely because she was a late riser. Then he realized that the door was locked. Phyllis had had the key but he managed to borrow a duplicate from the old woman who apparently lived in a cellar or hole in the basement of the building with the idea that she should act as an underpaid and overworked concierge.

He let himself in and saw Phyllis lying naked on her bed as if she were still asleep, but when he went up to her to call her name she did not reply, for her throat had been cut with such skill and strength that only one or two muscles at the back of her neck and the vertebrae were still unsevered, keeping her head in place. Naturally there had been an immense outpouring of blood which had stained the pillows and drenched the sheets as far down as her waist.

Bertram was chilled and horrified by what he saw and then asked himself the question: 'Why was she killed?' Very little was missing. A diary that she kept could not be found and a trinket that she sometimes wore, of very little value, was missing. Bertram called the police and the police doctor gave it as his opinion that she had been dead about four hours and that she had been killed in her sleep about three o'clock in the morning.

The case created a sensation. True, those connected with it were comparatively humble people and in the ordinary way, such was the social climate of the day, this would have made the murder obscure, but the circumstances were truly horrifying. Emily Dimmock had been young and very beautiful and the story that emerged as the police investigated the matter made it a fascinating and compulsive tale with a very wide appeal. It even confirmed in their belief the many millions of the public who believed that 'once a prostitute, always a prostitute', represented an eternal truth. Moreover, the young man who was eventually charged with the murder was so unusual a character, so talented and – horrifying though it may seem – so much fun, that his guilt or his innocence became a subject of intense national debate.

Of course, it was the fact that Bertram worked at night that made it almost impossible for Phyllis to break with her former life. Her profession had been a night profession. She had never 'worked' during the day – or very seldom. It was when the lights went on in London that she had emerged on to the street to decoy a man. Moreover, because she was young and beautiful, during the comparatively short time she had been a whore, she had collected a clientele of devoted patrons and they were insistent that she could have the best of both worlds. By all means let her marry the young cook if she wanted to, but as he was employed every night away from home why should she not enjoy the pleasure and reap the considerable rewards of her large and growing practice? And that, of course, is exactly what had in fact occurred.

The night before the murder Phyllis had been seen at a public house called the 'Eagle' with a young man whom witnesses described as looking poor, but intelligent, educated and genteel. Later the same night she was seen with a more formidable looking gentleman, apparently better off. Moreover, she had been seen with the genteel young man at another public house the 'Rising Sun', on two previous nights in the same week. This information was supplied to the police by a young ship's cook (we seem to be specializing in cooks in this story) who told the police that he was a friend of Phyllis and had, in fact, slept with her at 29 St Paul's Road on the two nights before the murder. On the night of the murder itself he had a watertight alibi that the police were completely unable to break and which, in fact, became stronger the more they investigated it.

A large number of young ladies in the same profession as Phyllis were questioned and said in effect: 'Oh, yes, there was a young man who was one of Phyllis's regulars. We remember him at the "Rising Sun". Gentleman he was, artist or something. . . .' This kind of evidence, coming from the source it did, presented the police with as many problems as it did clues. Could they trust what the girls said? How many men had Phyllis on her waiting list? Which of these had an overwhelming motive to murder her? Were they dealing with a crime of jealousy? A crime of passion? Or was there some other motive which had not even been dug up but remained obscurely buried in the smoky public houses of Camden Town and the cheap rented flatlets of this part of London?

Some of the evidence which the police had in a rapidly growing file pointed to a young artist named Robert Wood, who was employed by the Sand and Blast Manufacturing Company who had their offices and works in Grays Inn Road. Like everybody else in the district Robert Wood had gossiped about the murder with his friends, saying: 'No wonder the police can't discover who did it. These women never know whom they are taking home and they forget whom they have slept with after a few days.'

The police, however, did not despair because they had one good hard clue that they thought might lead them to the murderer. Hidden away in one of Phyllis's suitcases they had found a postcard. On one side of the postcard was a clever drawing of a woman with a child. On the other side there was a message, apparently from a woman, making a date. It said: 'Phyllis darling, If it pleases you, meet me at 8.15 at the . . . .' The message ended here with a sketch of a rising sun. The postcard ended with the words: 'Yours to a cinder, Alice.' The postcard was addressed to 'Mrs Bertram Shaw, 29 St Paul's Road, Camden Town'.

When the police had first arrived in the bedroom where Phyllis lay murdered they had noticed immediately that a postcard album was on the floor and that some postcards were missing. It rather looked as if the murderer had been interested in extracting a particular postcard but there was no means of telling whether he had found it or not. They did find the remnants of a letter which seemed to have been burnt but was in the same handwriting as that of the postcard.

Faced with all these difficulties the police decided to take an unusual step; unusual, that is, during the period we are speaking of. They decided to ask the help of the press and they published a facsimile of the postcard in the Sunday papers asking anyone who thought they knew the author of the postcard to contact them immediately.

The advertisement was successful. An artist's model named Ruby Young, again a girl of great beauty, had been seduced by a married doctor, which accounted for the fact that her family had disowned her (' never darken my doors again ') and she had been forced to earn her living as a model. Robert Wood had fallen in love with her and she had fallen in love with Robert Wood. He was a much better artist than his employment might suggest and several of the noted painters of the time had commented on his work, saying that it showed real promise. Both Robert Wood and Ruby Young came from the same background, which was intensely respectable and middle-class. It seems likely that Robert and Ruby would have married but Ruby persuaded herself, most unwisely, that she must make a clean breast of everything and she told Robert about the incident with the doctor, after which he decided not to marry her but to live with her, and he does not seem to have minded too much if she had other men friends who contributed to her support. There was no doubt whatever that Ruby was intensely jealous of Robert and that that jealousy had grown so hot about the time of the murder that it had led to a breach between them, possibly a temporary breach, but nevertheless a serious quarrel.

When Ruby Young saw the postcard in the Sunday newspapers she recognized it immediately as being Robert's work and then she remembered something strange. Just after the murder Robert had sent her a telegram asking her to meet him at a restaurant and the conversation that followed seemed to suggest that Robert was trying to establish an alibi through Ruby. At a later meeting Robert apparently said to Ruby: ' I am in real trouble ', and Ruby agreed, producing the newspaper cutting and adding: ' That is your handwriting.' At this second meeting Robert told Ruby that he had a complete explanation of what had happened. This was the explanation that he gave.

He had met Phyllis Dimmock at the ' Rising Sun ' on a Friday. They were sitting together on stools by the bar when a small boy came in selling postcards. Phyllis wanted to buy one but Robert had dissuaded her, saying that he had much better ones.

He then produced some postcards he happened to have with him which he had collected on a trip to Bruges. Phyllis had chosen the one of the woman and child. Robert then wrote the postcard and signed it ' Alice ' as a joke, but he did not give it to her, saying he would post it to her after he had decorated it. He did post it to her and she received it. Robert also said that this was to be the end of his association with Phyllis and that the postcard was intended to be a memento of their friendship.

Robert and Ruby went into much detail concerning a firm alibi for Robert on the fatal Wednesday night and Robert's brother, Charles, and his wife Bessie were brought into the matter, signing a document to back up the story, but the really weak link in the alibi was poor Ruby, who had not the strength of mind to stick to her story. The police visited her and threatened her and compelled her to help them. Acting on their instructions she made an assignation with Robert Wood in Grays Inn Road. She greeted him with a kiss. It was the salute of betrayal. A police officer, Inspector Neill, was following them at a discreet distance. Eventually he came up and arrested Robert, saying that he had evidence that he had written postcards to Phyllis Dimmock, the murdered woman, to which Robert replied: 'I only wrote one postcard.' Robert was not too concerned at this time, he still believed that Ruby would clear him.

When Robert Wood reached the police station he made a long statement based on the entirely false alibi which he had agreed with Ruby and which he thought Ruby would confirm. This monumental lie very nearly convicted him of a murder.

However, Robert Wood was a young man of great charm with a wide circle of friends who absolutely refused to believe that he could have committed this atrocious crime. It was, they said, contrary to his whole nature, which was gentle, artistic, intuitive and trusting. So they hired the services of Arthur Newton, a very well-known solicitor who, as soon as he had studied the papers, briefed Edward Marshall Hall, who had Wellesly-Orr as a junior in his chambers; Wellesly-Orr afterwards became the Stipendiary Magistrate in Manchester. It was a case after Marshall's own heart. It was possible to believe that

Robert Wood had got himself into this appalling mess by his own stupidity and that Phyllis had, in fact, been murdered by another man of a far more brutal and savage character who had taken her home on the night she had met her death, a man probably a pervert, certainly a sadist, perhaps a man suffering from some great feeling of injustice. Now, it so happened that one of the witnesses had mentioned that the night before the murder Phyllis, after leaving Robert Wood, had joined up with a lame man, whom she said she hated, but who was a man of exceptional strength and belonged to the London underworld of the time.

As had happened before in great murder cases, and will perhaps happen again, the police attempted to ' seal up ' the gaps in their evidence. For instance they produced a dust-cart man who said he had seen Robert leaving Phyllis's flat very early on the morning of the murder. Moreover he had caught sight of his face by the street lamp and had identified him by his peculiar walk. But Robert Wood did not really have any peculiarity either in the way he carried himself or the way he walked. Then the police remembered the lame man and Marshall Hall thought that he would be able to destroy the evidence of the dustman. To prevent this happening the police produced another prostitute known as ' May ' to confirm the evidence of the dustman. If anything this made matters worse for the prosecution, for it was clear that the police had tried to build up the dyke at the points where they thought it was most vulnerable.

The tragedy of this remarkable case was the fact that Robert could not believe that Ruby had been overcome by the threats of the police and when she gave her evidence, although it was clear that she still loved Robert Wood dearly, it was also clear that the two of them together had tried to establish a fraudulent alibi. Even so, the question remained, had they done this out of fear of publicity, which would certainly have resulted in Robert Wood losing his job, in fear of the police, or had they done it because in truth Robert Wood had murdered Phyllis Dimmock?

When this case came for trial it seemed that the young artist was in the greatest peril. If the police evidence was not broken down in important particulars, Robert Wood would hang.

At this point there was a consultation in chambers between the mercurial, brilliant leader, Marshall Hall, and his practical down-to-earth junior, Wellesly-Orr. Marshall thought that Wood was 'as mad as a hatter'. Marshall Hall's view was that if he was called Wood would hang himself. But Wellesly-Orr took the view that not to call him would be fatal. The very experienced solicitor, Arthur Newton, took the view that Robert Wood was too unreliable a man to put into the witness box.

The great case opened and Wellesly-Orr was still under the impression that his leader was not going to call the prisoner. Marshall, as usual, had bustled in very late, just before the appearance of the judge, just in time to take his seat and collect his brief and the array of pens and pencils which his clerk had set out for him. He beckoned to Wellesly-Orr, who sat just behind him, and whispered to him: 'I am going to call Wood. It is essential.' Wellesly-Orr nodded, realizing that some flash of intuition had told Marshall Hall that only by taking the jury completely into his confidence and by putting all his cards on the table would he be able to have a chance of acquitting his client.

This extraordinary case riveted the attention of the press both of England and the Empire. The trial took place before Mr Justice McCardie and Sir Charles Mathews was the leading counsel for the prosecution. Sir Charles was one of the most experienced criminal lawyers in the country and had the reputation of being a deadly prosecutor, the kind of reputation which Travers Humphreys was to gain a decade later.

Wood sat in the dock, apparently completely unconcerned with the dreadful drama that was enveloping him and being enacted before his eyes. During the opening of the prosecution case he amused himself by making sketches. This was at the time when there was a passion for diabolo and he made a sketch which he entitled 'Lady Diabolo of Monte Carlo' spinning her string, tossing one man after the other into the air so that they broke on the pavement. His sketches showed some kind of eccentric genius, so vivid and alive were they.

Marshall Hall could be a ferocious cross-examiner. Occasionally this was his undoing, but in the case of the ship's cook, who was a key witness against Robert Wood, he was extremely successful. He managed to make the cook admit that he knew the woman 'May' and moreover that May had given him a description of a young man who knew Phyllis. It was clear that it was from this description that he had picked out Robert Wood in identification parades. This was an absolutely vital point. It meant that he had not identified Wood because he had seen him but from a description that somebody else had given him. The cook was obviously petrified lest he himself should be regarded as the murderer and Marshall Hall tore his evidence up. Marshall Hall also put to the witness a short note signed 'Bert' making an appointment with Phyllis the day before the murder. Marshall Hall had been careful not to accuse the cook of murder but merely to discredit his evidence. After Marshall's cross-examination the cook was in such a state of dither and apparent terror that Sir Charles Mathews had some difficulty in restoring his credibility in a short re-examination.

It was on the second day of the trial that a fellow lodger of the ship's cook was called, and here again Marshall Hall was extremely successful. One of his key questions was: 'Did you hear that he [the ship's cook] slept with Dimmock on the Monday, Tuesday and Sunday nights?' The answer was: 'Yes.' Later the witness apparently realized the implication of this answer and tried to go back on it. Mr Justice McCardie, who throughout the trial seemed to take up an attitude hostile to the prisoner, said he had not heard it. This, of course, annoyed Marshall Hall, never the sweetest-tempered of men in court, and he called for the shorthand note which confirmed both the question and the answer. Marshall noticed that the jury had started to whisper among themselves, apparently impressed with the unreliability of the witnesses called by the Crown. By nature Marshall Hall was impetuous and he could easily have spoilt this advantage, but he noticed the jury's reaction and wisely pursued the matter no further.

The next witness to give his evidence was the cartman, and he had altered by nearly ten minutes the time at which he had said that he had seen Wood. Marshall Hall thought, possibly correctly, that he had done this in order to avoid the difficulty that, at the time put forward in his first statement, the street lamps had almost certainly been extinguished – and he had referred to the street lamp as helping him to see Wood more clearly.

On more than one occasion during the case Marshall Hall crossed swords with the judge; for instance when a young man who worked with Robert Wood gave evidence that he was of a gentle, quiet disposition, the judge interrupted by asking the witness: 'Did you know that he was leading this immoral life, sleeping with this woman?' Marshall Hall strenuously objected. There was no evidence that Robert Wood was immoral and, in any case, he was not charged with immorality. There was no conclusive evidence that he had slept with Phyllis and, again, this was not the subject of the investigation, but both allegations could greatly prejudice the jury. However, Mr Justice McCardie brushed Marshall aside and asked his questions, possibly putting up the backs of the jury by doing so.

Towards the end of the first week of the trial, five or six young prostitutes were called to give evidence concerning Robert Wood's association with Phyllis Dimmock. They appeared to be extremely unreliable witnesses and they showed a curious mixture of brazenness and fear. The London prostitutes at this time were a community to themselves, in the same way that the Jews were in the ghettos of Eastern Europe. There were about 80,000 of them in London and they did, of course, continue to parade the streets of the capital until Mr Butler, in a somewhat short-sighted burst of puritanical enthusiasm, drove them underground. In any case they made bad witnesses, touchy to a degree, and appearing to think that all questions were intended to discredit them personally. This enabled Marshall Hall to make steady progress in the case for the defence

A character known as 'Scotch Bob' flitted in and out of the evidence, but in the end he became so elusive that it seemed that there might be two of him and the jury gave the impression that they were discounting this evidence.

When the prosecution closed their case, Marshall Hall submitted that there was no case against Wood to go to the jury. Mr Justice McCardie, of course, held that there was a case for the jury to decide and in so deciding he was undoubtedly correct.

When Marshall Hall rose to address the jury for the first time he did so in a speech of such fervent eloquence that it is remembered to this day. I quote one passage which shows some of his ability and delicacy in entering into a rapport with the jury.

> Gentlemen, in the last three days you may have thought that, now and then, I was pressing a witness unfairly, that I urged an unfair advantage, that I asked an unworthy question. If I seemed to exceed the proper limits, gentlemen, I implore you to forgive me; but, after all, why should not I have? My whole anxiety was for my client. Gentlemen, his life is at stake. I cannot rob the witness for the prosecution of that. They have far less to lose at my hands than he has at yours. Gentlemen, this burden has been lying very heavily on my shoulders. It will pass to yours all too soon.

On the whole, and against expectation, the defence witnesses stood up well in the witness box. There was Robert's father, a forthright old Scotsman, Charles Wood, a half-brother, and a man called Rogers, who was a jeweller and who had a most peculiar walk which he demonstrated for the jury, thus casting doubt on the identification of 'the man with the limp'.

The highlight of the trial was, of course, the evidence of Robert Wood himself, and he was for Marshall Hall a most disconcerting witness. He just seemed incapable of giving a straight answer to a straight question. His colourful and curious mind would dart off like a butterfly in pursuit of some whimsy that had very little or no bearing on the question put to him. However, although Wood was a very unsatisfactory witness it did seem almost impossible to regard him as the savage brute who had slit the throat of Phyllis Dimmock, and perhaps it was this that helped him most. Sir Charles Mathews gave Wood a terrible time in the box. Sir Charles belonged to the old school of criminal prosecutor and gave the impression that he represented God and the witness represented the Devil. Perhaps he was getting a little out-of-date and overdid his act. In any case, although Wood had been irritatingly elusive with Marshall Hall, now Sir Charles Mathews found it equally difficult to pin him down.

Sir Charles Mathews met with some success when he put the postcard to Robert Wood, but when it came to the crucial matter of whether he had been with Phyllis on the night before the murder, Wood gave a steady answer that appeared to ring true. On the whole Marshall and Wellesly-Orr could give a sigh of relief when Robert Wood returned from the witness box to the dock. He had not been broken. He had not been entirely discredited, and the impression that he was incapable of brutal murder had, if anything, increased. The view of those in court was that Robert Wood could not by nature have committed this particular crime unless he was mad – and he was not mad. He was just a rather silly and very gifted young man.

In his final speech Marshall Hall was at his best, reserving the rhetoric for the very end and compelling himself to treat each issue in the case logically and consecutively in the body of his speech. Marshall's plea was summed up in his words: 'What is the evidence of murder? The only iota of evidence against the man is that of a cartman. If any of you, gentlemen, had a suffering animal to kill, and whether you killed it or not depended on this cartman's evidence, would you kill it?'

Marshall Hall managed to have a real court room flare-up with Sir Charles Mathews by suggesting that Sir Charles had not called two witnesses for the Crown who should have been called. It was a storm in a bitter teacup. Finally the great trial drew to its close and the jury settled themselves to listen to the last address of this astoundingly handsome and compelling figure who seemed literally to have thrown the cloak of his own integrity round the prisoner to save him from the gallows.

I have nothing more to say than to remind you that now the responsibility is yours, not mine. If you are satisfied beyond all reasonable doubt that the man standing there murdered Emily

Dimmock, though it breaks your hearts to do it, find him guilty and send him to the gallows. But, if, under the guidance of a greater than any earthly power, making up your minds for yourselves upon this matter, if you feel you cannot truthfully and conscientiously say you are satisfied that the prosecution have proved that this man is guilty, then, I say, it is your duty, as it must be your pleasure, to say that Robert Wood did not murder Emily Dimmock.

As the great advocate finished his speech a fitful winter sun shone through the high windows of the Old Bailey and illuminated his features. It almost seemed as if Marshall had the elements at his command.

Mr Justice McCardie summed up heavily against the prisoner, of whose guilt he appeared to be completely convinced. However, at the very end of his summing up he relented somewhat and directed the jury that if they thought the evidence inconclusive they should give the prisoner the benefit of the doubt. The extraordinary about-turn of attitude of the judge is difficult to explain, for, at the very end, he appeared to be inviting the jury to acquit Robert Wood. Is it possible that even the judge, veteran lawyer that he was, had at last been persuaded by the vehemence and sincerity of Marshall Hall?

Everyone expected the jury to be out for not less than an hour and possibly for some hours, but they returned in less than twenty minutes. There was a buzz of intense excitement in the court. The judge was recalled and the clerk put the question to the foreman of the jury: 'Do you find Robert Wood guilty of murder as charged?'

The answer was: 'Not Guilty.' There was a roar of applause from the court which had to be quelled.

What happened to Robert Wood? We do not know, but years later Sir Edward Marshall Hall, as he had become, was accosted by a smart and obviously prosperous middle-aged man as he came down the steps of an assize court. The man said to him: 'You don't know me, Sir Edward?' Marshall Hall replied: 'I have a terrible memory for faces, but wait a minute, isn't your name Wood?' The man replied: 'No, that's not my name, but I thought you might like to know that I am doing all right, and that I am still grateful to you after all these years.'

The Camden Town murder will never be forgotten. It was one of the most remarkable criminal trials of the Edwardian age.

3

Murder For Money

Ever since man gave up the civilized and reasonable way of life founded on barter, the fair exchange of property for property, we have been in difficulties and in danger. As soon as money was made the symbol not only of exchange but of power, and wealth, and prestige, it was inevitable that the new god would replace the old gods and that eventually all standards would be debased.

Money has split the world into two camps: the capitalists, who may seek to curb the power of money but end in waging a war in its defence, and the communists whose whole philosophy is founded not so much on any desire for equality – Russian officials are among the most pampered and privileged in the world – as on a determination to prevent the rise of a class of rich men with corresponding power. Founded, that is to say, on envy and fear.

Having invented money we cannot control it. The whole structure of exchange, international banking and balance of payments is in constant chaos and a source of danger to international peace in countries like Britain and America, whose economies are always teetering between prosperity and disaster.

Money, moreover, has created the new imperialism. Russia has conquered and subdued seven middle-European countries, from the Baltic to the borders of Greece, in a naked and terrible aggression which neither Hungary nor Czechoslovakia will ever forget, so burnt is it into the memories of the people. Money, in the form of land and rice and markets, has driven the Chinese to pursue a course of imperialist aggression that the Chinese emperors in their wisdom never embarked upon, until now the whole of South-East Asia trembles before the onslaught by open attack or subversion, or steels itself in defence.

Nor has money brought internal blessings to rich countries. In the United States vast areas of rat-infested slums disfigure the great cities, while even in advanced countries, such as South Africa, the standard of living of the majority, though notably higher than the rest of Africa, leaves much to be desired. The golden dreams never seem to come true. Those who lavish money in 'aid' to the poorer nations are invariably met by abuse and cringing demands for more and more. Money pollutes. Money corrodes. Yet we cannot do without it. Having made our decision there is no going back. We have to cope as best we can.

If this is the result of money on a large canvas we must admit that it has enabled great humanitarian enterprises to be launched. But it has also made it possible to indulge in unbelievable evil. We have by its aid reached the stars. At the same time we have invented a means of destroying civilization overnight. On balance, has it been worth it?

Money has almost driven religion out of business except in those portions of the earth where the Roman Catholic Church is strong, or where Buddhism or the Moslem faith have a real grip on believers. In Europe, in particular, Christianity appears to be dying in Britain, Scandinavia, France, Germany and Italy, while the communist regimes, of course, crush any faith that they fear might compete with their own for the minds of men.

Perhaps the evil that money can do is seen even more vividly if we bring the camera in very close and examine the mind and motives of one man. We know that men will work for money, live for money, die for money. But what kind of a man is it that will take the life of another for money? What kind of a man is it that will murder solely for money?

The answer, I think, often is that it is a man whose business all his life has been the collection and handling of money. Men who are very close to the contagion of money, who handle it daily, sometimes end up by worshipping it. They may not actually get down on their knees and pray to their golden god but, in fact, in their hearts and mind only money motivates.

All they do is explicable only in terms of cash. The transfer of money from other persons to themselves is the mainspring of their lives. This is the ultimate corruption, and it is this that makes them capable of murder if thereby they think they can enrich themselves.

Such a man was Frederick Henry Seddon, an insurance agent. Everything the world knew of Henry Seddon was to his credit, if one accepted the standards of 1910 and the admiration which the public had for the poor boy who had made good. Seddon had started at the age of eighteen with the London & Manchester Industrial Insurance Company. He received a pittance as an office boy, making the tea, even brushing out the office. He was there at seven before the staff arrived and was not allowed to leave until six when the last clerk had left. But he did not waste his time. Actuarial figures fascinated him and long before he was elevated from office boy to junior clerk he could tell you from memory what the premium payable on £1,000 of life insurance at the age of thirty-five would be, or what the annuity payment on a similar amount at the age of sixty-five would fetch. He was never bored. Money fascinated him. He found it much more enthralling than the pastimes in which most of the young men indulged. He began to climb the ladder of his firm. His inferiors did not like him because he did not spare them, but his superiors saw in him a dedicated and trustworthy servant and promotion came his way.

However, in these days before the First World War, companies like London & Manchester Industrial Insurance expected to buy a man's total work and devotion for a very modest wage even after twenty years of service, and it was only by showing great ingenuity in saving and by cutting expenses to a bare minimum that Seddon at forty had managed to become a man of modest property. He had saved money and managed to obtain from it an income of nearly four hundred pounds a year. He had also bought, after protracted – and somewhat acrimonious – negotiations, 63 Tollington Park, which was too big for him and his wife. He had married a Lancashire woman who was as good at 'managing' as he was and they had four children. Seddon was now quite a figure at his Masonic Lodge and seemed to enjoy the tribal mumbo-jumbo of Masonic ritual. He was also a pillar of his chapel. Very much a pillar of the Establishment, a man on his way up, was Frederick Henry Seddon.

The thought of the three empty rooms at his home naturally preyed on Seddon's mind, for surely he could let these rooms for money? He advertised for a lodger and, as a result, Eliza Barrow and her small nephew, Ernest Grant, came and stayed with the Seddons, paying rent for their rooms. Financially it was a satisfactory arrangement, but there were drawbacks. Eliza Barrow was bedridden, and most unappetizing. She smelt because she was too lazy to wash, she constantly picked her nose and from time to time she urinated in her bed. She took constant medicine for her multiple ailments, some of which were real and others fanciful. She was also a miser and mean and avaricious to a startling degree.

However Eliza Barrow, who came of a much better family than the Seddons, paid her rent on the nail, and little inconveniences such as the odour that came from her bedroom and the flies that increasingly collected around her had to be put up with. You don't make money for nothing.

Eliza Barrow had a 'fortune' of some £3,000 invested mainly in East India stock which was not giving a good return at this time. Seddon viewed his lodger with an experienced and calculating eye. Seddon saw at once that Miss Barrow was genuinely ill, so that there could be no question of doing life insurance business with her. But what about an annuity? That might be quite a business. In return for the £3,000 the company could offer her about £150 a year, which was more than she was receiving from her stocks. And how long was she likely to live? Seddon considered her life expectation very carefully and decided that, one way or another, it might be much less than the actuarial figures suggested. On her 'bad days' Eliza seemed already to have the mask and pallor of death upon her and Seddon, who knew that look, decided that he might, after establishing himself as her unofficial financial adviser, put the proposal of an annuity to her. The commission on annuity work was good. Seddon and

Eliza had many talks in the fly-infested bedroom and they enjoyed them. Both had the same over-riding passion: money, money, money. Eliza saw herself as the cleverer of the two, an assumption that Seddon did nothing to dispel, but he baited the annuity hook very cunningly with greed in the form of increased income and in the end Eliza swallowed the bait – and the hook.

In addition to handing over to Seddon the money she took out of the East India stock, Miss Barrow decided to take home certain bank savings because she was acutely worried by rumours that she had heard concerning the stability of the London & Finsbury Savings Bank. The rumours were quite groundless and we do not know who suggested them to Eliza. It may have been Seddon, but we have no evidence that it was. The result was that she had some hundreds of pounds in gold hidden in her room. Eliza Barrow was beginning to present great temptations to Henry Seddon.

Before coming to the Seddons Eliza Barrow had stayed for a considerable time with her own relatives, Mr and Mrs Vonderahe. They had managed to part with their quarrelsome cousin on good terms and there is no doubt that they regarded themselves as her heirs should 'anything happen to her'. Little did they know.

Eliza Barrow, worried and distraught and feeling most unwell, decided to make a new will. The trusted and clever Mr Seddon was made sole executor and the sole beneficiary was not the Vonderahes, but little Ernest Grant.

Eliza now became much worse and Mrs Seddon had to nurse her most of the time. Her doctor thought that she was getting gradually worse with heart, stomach and liver trouble. He doubted whether much could be done, though he expected her to linger on for some years, sustained by greed and her intense interest in her own affairs.

Seddon, when he had completed the annuity business, paid the first instalment to Eliza in gold. That pleased her very much – one hundred and fifty gleaming golden sovereigns. But the cash payment was curious and perhaps ominous. There was some evidence that Seddon had not passed the business on to his firm – yet. Did he intend, if Miss Barrow were to die, to keep her entire fortune himself?

She did die one night in agony, complaining of acute stomach pain. Mrs Seddon sat up with her while Seddon sat outside the room, close at hand in the event of anything going wrong. As soon as Eliza expired Seddon rang her doctor, who issued a certificate that she had died of endemic diarrhoea, without troubling to call round or see the body. In his mind Eliza had probably died of very natural causes. It was a pity he did not look in for he might have asked a few questions. He might have taken a sample of the old woman's vomiting that still clung to her sheets – and he might have noticed the flypapers soaked in water that apparently had been waging an unsuccessful war with the flies.*

So Seddon felt that the all-clear had been given. He arranged for a most economical funeral, ignoring Eliza's wish that she should be buried in the family vault, and he did not trouble to inform the Vonderahes of the tragedy. Instead Seddon took his wife and little Ernest Grant on a fortnight's holiday at Southend. They enjoyed it.

While the Seddons and little Ernie were having their first carefree holiday at Southend for over two years, back at home things were starting to go amiss for Seddon. Those cousins, the Vonderahes, had heard of the death of Eliza and thought it odd that Mr Seddon had not troubled to inform them of it. Eliza had been collected from her cousins' house, so the Seddons knew quite well who her only relatives were and where they lived. The Vonderahes made some enquiries and nothing they learnt made them any happier. When they discovered that their cousin's fortune had vanished, all apparently to Henry Seddon, they were very upset indeed. They made a complaint to the police, who asked for an order to exhume the body. This was granted and the Home Office pathologist found over two grains of arsenic in the dead woman's stomach and other organs. Moreover, the

*Fly-papers usually contain a high concentration of arsenic.

police discovered that Maggie Seddon, a small daughter, had been sent out by the Seddons to buy fly papers some time before the tragedy.

The case came before the coroner and, knowing that he must be a witness, Seddon went round to see a young lawyer whom he knew and who lived near him – a Mr Saint. Seddon did not take the matter too seriously: 'An old girl who was a lodger of ours has died and they've apparently found some poison in her stomach. I want you to appear for me.'

Mr Saint agreed to represent Mr Seddon and, for once, Seddon did not quibble about the fee. The coroner's inquest found that Miss Barrow had died of arsenical poisoning accentuating a chronic stomach condition. The Seddons were both arrested during the inquest.

When Seddon was arrested he said: 'How terrible. None of my family have been concerned with murder. Are you arresting my wife? Have they found arsenic in the body?' There were two interpretations to be put on this. Either it was the carelessness of innocence, or it was the blundering, surprised indication of guilt.

A great criminal trial was now looming, in some ways the greatest murder case of all time. Mr Saint hastily briefed Mr Rentoul, an up-and-coming junior barrister and asked him whom he would like to have as a leader. Mr Rentoul asked whether he could have anyone. And the answer was: 'Yes.' Mr Seddon had decided to disburse some of his painfully collected savings. Young Rentoul had no doubt as to whom he wanted to be led by. 'Then we must have Marshall Hall,' he said.

Edward Marshall Hall, KC, was just starting the most spectacular period of his career as a great advocate most famous for his defence in murder cases. I met 'Marshall' twice, once in Exeter at assizes when my father was on the grand jury, and once in Manchester when I was a very young barrister attending Bar mess on circuit. He was a magnificent-looking man, six-foot-three, with bold, straight gestures, blue eyes and a mane of white hair which had been light brown or golden. He looked like a legendary Viking hero. He was a most attractive person, impulsive, loyal and generous. And he was the greatest emotional advocate of his day who, given half a chance, could sweep a jury off their feet by the electric force of his personality and his pulverizing eloquence. If anyone could free the Seddons it was 'Marshall'.

It is often said that advocates of the type of Edward Marshall Hall would not be effective in the more pragmatic and quieter atmosphere of the law courts today, with the judges looking like civil servants and the barristers like slightly superior clerks. I think this is a complete delusion. If the death penalty is restored – and there seems to be overwhelming support for its restoration to beat the gangs who carry guns without it – I am sure that Marshall Hall would dominate the number one criminal court today just as he dominated the Old Bailey at the trial of the Seddons. For his appeal was not only to the heart. He brought his great gifts to bear on all the facts of the case and in this case, in particular, his very wide medical knowledge and his special knowledge of poisons enabled him to set up exactly the same kind of defence which juries today would listen to with respect and attention.

Marshall led Mr Rentoul, who himself appeared for Mrs Seddon, but in fact Marshall conducted the whole defence of the Seddons, taking the case of Mrs Seddon in his stride. The evidence against Mrs Seddon was not so black as that against her husband, but the jury might think that she must have known what was going on and she, too, was in dire danger.

Sir Rufus Isaacs, the Attorney-General, prosecuted, and no abler man has ever held that office. He spoke calmly, quietly, with deliberation. He was the master of clear, chronological presentation. Without indulging in any vehemence, in his opening speech he conveyed the entire picture and when he sat down there seemed to be no escape for either Seddon or his wife.

However, he had had to formulate a theory of what, exactly, Miss Barrow had died of. The doctor had given his certificate and said that, though he had not paid a visit after death, he had based his finding on attending the dead woman, who had a condition which made such a death likely if not inevitable. But the prosecution was going to call Sir William Wilcox, the noted Home Office pathologist, to say that Miss Barrow had died of 'acute' arsenical poisoning, that a massive overdose had been administered within twenty-four hours of death. Just over two grains had been found, just enough to kill her, but Sir William estimated that arsenic passes through the system so quickly that something like five grains must have been taken.

No one, of course, had seen any arsenic administered at all. Was it possible that this disagreeable, confused old woman had drunk some of the water in which the fly-papers had been soaked, accidentally or on purpose? She was very secretive. Was it possible that she had been taking arsenic for a long period? If she had, the prosecution case fell to the ground. If Marshall Hall could show that she had died of 'chronic' arsenical poisoning Seddon might escape, for she had not been with the Seddons long enough to develop chronic poisoning. This was, as the case developed, seen to be the crux of the dispute. The case lasted ten days, an extraordinary length of time for a murder charge. And it was a hard battle all the way.

The fiercest fought duel of the whole trial was between Sir William Wilcox and Marshall Hall, when the great advocate rose to cross-examine the pathologist. Marshall's cross-examination raised two major points. First he pointed out that the amount of arsenic found in the stomach was .63 of a grain and that this was made up to over two grains by a calculation of the arsenic that was likely to be dispersed in other organs where it could not be weighed as the contents of the stomach could be.

Marsh's test, as it was called, was ingenious and usually remarkably accurate, but it had this defect: if there was only a small miscalculation in the original estimate that mistake could be multiplied many times when the test was applied. The two men tore at this bone, and Marshall's mastery of the theory and practise of arsenical poisoning was seen to be a match for Sir William.

The second very important point that Marshall made concerned the very minute quantities of arsenic said to have been found in the dead woman's hair, both the proximal hair and the 'distal' ends of the hair. Marshall got an admission from the witness that he had found minute quantities of arsenic in both. Then Sir William realized what he had said: If arsenic was in the hair, even in the long hair, Eliza Barrow must have been taking arsenic for months, possibly for years. Towards the end of his cross-examination he thought of an explanation. The coffin had been smeared with fluid from the woman's body and with blood as well. Her hair had caught the arsenical traces from this excreta. Sir William repeated that he was quite sure that Miss Barrow had died of a massive overdose shortly before her death.

Seddon did not make a good witness. His answers were clever but the greed of the man shone through. The meanness of his mind was plain for the jury to see. Sir Rufus asked him a famous first question. Having established how long Eliza Barrow had been with the Seddons he said:

'Did you like her?'

Seddon was taken off balance. 'Did I like her?' he said. 'Yes. that was the question.'

Then the ready wit comes back and Seddon answered: 'She was not the kind of woman you could fall in love with, but I deeply sympathized with her.'

It reminded one of Sir Edward Carson's famous first question to Oscar Wilde: 'How old are you?' And the vain Wilde was trapped into an unnecessary but ominous lie.

The Attorney-General put the facts of Miss Barrow's money to Seddon: the considerable fortune she had had when she came to lodge with them had vanished. Only ten pounds in gold and sixteen pounds' worth of possessions remained when she died. There could be little doubt that Seddon had robbed her. But had he murdered her? Views on this famous case are divided. There are those who think that Seddon was rightly convicted, and those who incline to the view that the prosecution did not prove their case beyond all reasonable doubt. What really happened was that Seddon, under the quiet but relentless cross-examination of Sir Rufus Isaacs, slowly but surely coiled the rope around his own neck. Gradually, in question after question, his utter absorption in the pursuit of money, regardless of any other consideration in the world, became painfully apparent. The jury, who seemed to have been impressed by Marshall's cross-examination of Sir William Wilcox, were seen to show antipathy to Seddon as his real character was exposed. His wife was very loyal to him, but she gave the impression of being a prematurely aged drudge who had been used by Seddon to bear the children and keep house. 'He never told me things,' she said.

The identification of 'Little Maggie', who was said to have been sent out to buy the fly-papers, was far from satisfactory, and the story of Seddon being seen by two of his workers 'counting the gold' after Miss Barrow had died seems a little far-fetched. Seddon was not liked by his colleagues. But he was a clever, careful man, hardly likely to count the dead woman's gold in public when he could so easily have done it privately.

It was Seddon, himself, who was his own executioner. As the drama rose to its climax, Sir Edward, who was suffering acutely from his back complaint, delivered one of the most outstanding speeches ever made in defence of a prisoner on a capital charge.

People do not commit murder for thirty shillings a week. If this man and this woman are guilty of this crime as charged, they have been guilty of almost diabolical cruelty. They sat with her, it is said, not to nurse her, but with cold-blooded, calculating patience watching her die and even giving her palliatives to simulate a natural death. It is outside the accepted behaviour of human beings. One would have to search the annals of the old Italian poisoners for any parallel.

The scientists have given us much but they have never been able to replace the vital spark we call life. You are asked to return a verdict of guilty in a case where there must always be a doubt when this case is debated in the years to come. We will never be certain that for long before her death, in some way, arsenic was finding its way into the body of this woman. Opportunity and motive are not enough. There must be proof.

If, by your verdict, you put out the spark of life in this man and if, indeed, a mistake is made, no power on earth can ever give him back his life.

Marshall's great speech was certainly necessary. Rufus Isaacs had made a very long speech, step by step piling up the evidence and, as the speech reached its climax, that beautiful, silken voice, never raised, appeared even more menacing.

Seddon had been tempted by the immediate prospect of, to him, a large sum in cash. Why had he not told the Vonderahes of their cousin's death? Seddon said he had written to them. He had carefully kept a copy of such a letter. It had not arrived.

The post at this time was a great deal better than it is today, fifty years later. The non-arrival of any letter the following day was a most unusual occurrence, the subject of a serious investigation. He had never sent the letter. He was just 'keeping his files in order'. Moreover little Ernest Grant had been whisked off to Southend. Why? Because he went to the same school as the Vonderahe children and might have talked.

The Attorney-General said that apart from seeing Seddon feeding the bedridden old women with arsenic, the jury could not have more conclusive evidence.

However, he did leave them a loophole in the case of Mrs Seddon. 'If you have no doubt that the man is guilty but you are not completely satisfied with the evidence against the woman. If you think that the evidence against her falls just short of that which the law requires then you would acquit her.'

This was remarkably helpful to Mrs Seddon. It certainly reflected the unspoken wish of the watching public. The thought of this wretched woman, who had been completely dominated by her monstrous husband, being suffocated to death or having her neck broken by the rope was unbearable to those who watched this truly historic trial.

The jury were out for an hour. They found Seddon guilty. There was an awful suspense before they found Mrs Seddon not guilty. Seddon moved to his wife and kissed her warmly. This gesture, apparently the first uncalculating and unrehearsed action of his during the whole trial, had an extraordinary effect on the public, many of the women weeping.

Before being sentenced in capital charges, the prisoner is

always asked if he has anything to say. The response is usually one word – ' No '.

But Seddon produced some notes from his pocket and made an excellent speech in which he denied absolutely that either he or his wife had ever given Eliza Barrow poison. Business was business, but murder was murder, something entirely different and evil. They had never contemplated it, far less carried it out. They had tried to persuade the old woman to go to hospital but she had refused, saying: ' You are my only friends.' They were the victims of an appalling set of circumstances and on this circumstantial evidence the jury, in the best of faith, had found an innocent man guilty . . . .

Mr Justice Bucknill was not one of the fierce, even arrogant judges of the Edwardian time. He was a cultured and humane man – and he was a Mason. At the end of his speech Seddon, also, as we have seen, a Mason, said: ' Before the Great Architect of the Universe I am not guilty, My Lord.' Then he made the Masonic sign.

This greatly upset the judge and he had to pause for a time before nerving himself to pass the awful sentence of death.

So Henry Seddon was led away to be hanged by the neck until he was dead. His wife was overcome with grief. She had loved the man.

Was Seddon rightly convicted? I am sure he committed this awful crime, but I do not think the evidence was conclusive. There was and always will be a doubt. The evidence of prolonged arsenical poisoning was nearly as strong as that in favour of a massive dose as the cause of death. The identification of 'Maggie ' buying the fly-papers was unsatisfactory. The amount of arsenic actually found in her stomach was less than a minimum fatal dose. Could not her doctor have been right in his diagnosis of the cause of death? But if the verdict had been not guilty then a very evil man, as satanic and as cruel as any criminal this century, would have gone free.

Mrs Seddon asked for her husband's body. The law refused.

I am glad that Mrs Seddon got off. She must have suspected that her husband was after the ' old girl's money ' and would do anything to get it, but she was a loyal woman and perhaps because of the children he had given her and she had given him, and their early struggles together, this terrible and sinister case is illumined by the one touching spectacle of a man and a woman clinging to each other till the end.

4
The Decent Inn of Death

The Americans and the British are far too closely related to see eye to eye on many of those intractable questions that seem to plague international affairs these days, but there is one sphere where, though jealousies are energetically maintained, they react with predictable conservatism and insularity.

British and American missionaries are, generally speaking, quite sure that the message of Christ is infinitely superior to the message of Buddha or Mohammed and in their secret hearts they regard the followers of these great faiths as 'heathens'. Of course, on the surface, it is all smooth persuasion and indirect suggestion, but there is no doubt about their underlying conviction that they offer salvation to those not yet received into the fold. The Catholics, of course, go a little further and have an eye open for the conversion of non-Catholic Christians as well, for only by embracing the original mother church of Christianity can a man or a woman receive the assured benediction of Rome.

Although this is true – or is as nearly true as generalizations usually are – we must make an exception in the case of medical missionaries. Many of these men were and are Americans, and in Siam, at any rate, their degrees were not of the standard that is now accepted. But they were dedicated, they often had great compassion. They spoke the language and the people loved them. In northern Siam in the year 1906 there was a strong American Mission in the principality of Chiengmai which was dominated by one man, whom everyone in the north knew as Father Ignatius. Father Ignatius was not an American. He was a Dane and he spoke English with that attractive sing-song melodiousness that the Danes never quite seem to lose. He spoke Siamese like a native, or rather that branch of the Thai language which was used by the Siamese people of the north, the Lao people, who formed the population of Chiengmai, the northern capital.

Father Ignatius was not too interested in saving people's bodies. That task he left to the great Dr Wallace whose fame as a healer was known all over the north. Father Ignatius was after men's souls.

When ten years earlier Father Ignatius had arrived in the wonderful country of northern Siam with its teak forests, its sapphire and ruby mines, its great rivers and rice fields and its gentle and happy people, he had been appalled by the fact that the Buddhist faith was accepted with absolute conviction by the entire population. There were virtually no converts and the Mission had given up its religious mission and directed its energy to saving men through medicine and medical care, which was the province of Dr Wallace.

Father Ignatius, who was an energetic and attractive man, decided to change all this. But he realized that, before he could hope to introduce a new faith, he must discover what the opposition consisted of, what in essence the old faith was, what it was that made the Buddhist way of life so strong in apparently giving the people hope as well as assurance.

He read voraciously and was first fascinated by the very beginning of the story. In the English translation of a book by Phya Apaiwongse on the origin of Buddhism he read:

Concerning the young prince, who was named Siddhartha, but who is often called after his family name Gautama or Sakyamuni (Sanskrit, *muni*, a 'solitary'), it is declared that though surrounded with luxury he gave such evidence of a contemplative disposition that his father, to prevent his embracing a religious life, i.e. that of a wandering mendicant, caused him to be married at an early age to a beautiful princess, and endeavoured to divert his mind from such a purpose by all the means at his command. For a time these efforts succeeded, and the young Siddhartha spent some years in soft luxurious enjoyment, until the subjects of his father began to fear that their future ruler would lack the vigour necessary for his position. At the age of twenty-six, however, he was awakened from his dreams of indolence and pleasure by the sight of a man in extreme old age, of another suffering from leprosy, of a corpse in the process of decay, and after these of an ascetic, or religious mendicant. The unsatisfying and fleeting character of all human enjoyment became deeply impressed upon his mind. His former questionings concerning the problems of human life now returned with renewed force, and after a severe mental struggle, he determined to solve the mystery, even at the cost of all that ambition, affection, or pleasure could offer. To effect this resolve he fled by night from his father's house, without even bidding farewell to his wife and newly-born son, and after divesting himself of his robes and cutting off his long hair, he embraced the life of a religious recluse.

Then he read all about the four sublime verities, which were said to be:

I That misery always accompanies existence
II That all modes of existence result from desire
III In Nirvana all pain and sorrow cease
IV There is a fourfold way leading to Nirvana

Finally he was fascinated by a poem ascribed to the Buddha himself, that had been translated by Mr Rhys David in his book on Buddhism.

In answer to the question, Which is the greatest blessing? Buddha replies:

Not to serve the foolish
But to serve the wise,
To honour those worthy of honour;
This is the greatest blessing.

To dwell in a pleasant land,
To have done good deeds in a former birth,
To have right desires for oneself;
This is the greatest blessing.

Much insight and education,
Self-control and pleasant speech,
And whatever word is well spoken;
This is the greatest blessing.

To support father and mother,
To cherish wife and child,
To follow a peaceful calling;
This is the greatest blessing.

To bestow alms and live righteously,
To give help to kindred,
Deeds which cannot be blamed;
This is the greatest blessing.

To abhor and cease from sin,
To eschew strong drink,
Not to be weary in well-doing;
This is the greatest blessing.

Reverence and lowliness,
Contentment and gratitude,
The hearing of the Law at due seasons;
This is the greatest blessing.

To be long-suffering and meek,
To associate with the members of the Sangha,
Religious talk at due seasons;
This is the greatest blessing.

Temperance and chastity,
A conviction of the four great truths,
The hope of Nirvana;
This is the greatest blessing.

Beneath the stroke of life's changes,
The mind that is unshaken,
Without anguish and passion, and secure;
This is the greatest blessing.

On every side are invincible
They who do acts like these.
On every side they walk in safety;
And this is the greatest blessing.

Father Ignatius realized when he had finished his studies that he had a real challenge to meet. He thought the matter over for months, considering how he should present the case for Christ to these unsophisticated, but often clever people. At first he thought that Buddhism lacked heart. That it did not have compassion, merely concentrating on the individual achieving a state of isolated serenity and perfection. But it soon became clear to him that Buddha had not been insensitive to the tears of the world.

The real attack, Father Ignatius decided, should be on this curious belief that on death the spirit fled the body to take up its residence eventually in another body and not, apparently, even a human body. This idea appalled Father Ignatius. The thought that he himself might one day become an ass was abhorrent. This was why the Buddhists burnt their dead, of course. The spirit had already departed so the sooner the corpse was consumed by the flames the better. It was true that the Prince of Chiengmai had kept a favourite wife for six months before the cremation ceremonies, but then royalty is always different, and one has to make allowances for protocol.

Burial was what Father Ignatius approved of. Decent deliberate burial with all the awful solemnity of the occasion. It was burial that his Viking ancestors had made into a great ritual and it was Christian burial that Father Ignatius practised in Chiengmai in the Protestant cemetery whenever he had a chance, intoning the dread words with a relish and a power that was deeply impressive. ' Dust to dust. Ashes to ashes.' When Father Ignatius conducted your funeral service you really had been well and truly laid to rest.

Father Ignatius always contrived that the funeral processions to the cemetery should be as long and as impressive as possible, for the Lao people who were well-mannered by nature and had respect and reverence for the dead, would kneel at the side of the road as the carriages and the hearses, loaded with orchids, passed by. A really good funeral was for Father Ignatius a public relations exercise as well as a religious duty. It enabled the people to see how these things should be done.

Unfortunately quite near the Protestant cemetery a Buddhist temple – Wat Saket – shone defiantly in the sunshine, its gilded spires flashing a message to the sun and the pagoda roofs of gold, indigo, green and red, receiving a message back. Cremations were always going on there and, attracted by the faint but unmistakable odour of burning flesh, a clutch of vultures hovered near by, while hawks from the Mei Ping river circled ominously in the intense blue sky above.

Sometimes when Father Ignatius was conducting a service two or three vultures, in an inquisitive way, would hop to the outskirts of the group round the grave and their expressions, in the imagination of Father Ignatius, seemed sardonic. However, the graves were never disturbed and there was no doubt that Father Ignatius's funerals were putting on a brave and a bold show. It was a case of Onward Christian Soldiers. Unfortunately the red line was very thin and was always in danger of being engulfed by the yellow sea of the Buddhist faithful, on whom Father Ignatius, year after year, failed to make much impression.

He had his faithful little band of followers however. There was the mission itself. There was a staff of five at the British Consulate (where Her Britannic Majesty's Government maintained three working elephants) and there were the 'teak-wallahs', the young men in the Borneo Company and the Bombay Burma Corporation, who on Christmas Day and at Easter would sober up in order to come to church and give Father Ignatius the support which was his due.

Apart from these certified Christians whose souls were firmly in the hands of Father Ignatius, and for whom, in the unfortunate event of their meeting an untimely death, Father Ignatius would put on a really fine funeral, there were some people whom Father Ignatius thought of in his mind as 'border people'. For instance, there was Chow Rart. What was the real position of Chow Rart? Was he a Christian as Father Ignatius hoped, or was he still, underneath, a Buddhist? Chow Rart, who was a poor and very distant relative of the Prince of Chiengmai (by a minor wife), had accepted a job as Director of the Mission, which meant that he supervised the office and was responsible for the Mission purchasing programme, the organization of journeys into the interior, the accounts, and a great many smaller matters of daily routine. Chow Rart was invaluable. His link with the Prince gave him a prestige throughout the north that no official body, and certainly no foreign power, could bestow. And he worked so well, seeming to enter into the enthusiasm of the young missionaries and being thoughtful and even respectful towards Father Ignatius and Dr Wallace and their families.

For all this he was paid about eight hundred *baht* a month, about £1,000 a year, which, in the north, made him a comparatively rich man. He was the golden apple of Father Ignatius's eye.

Father Ignatius did not quite retain the immense energy and enthusiasm that he had had when he first entered the field. He realized, but never admitted, that he was fighting a losing battle. But he fought it with defiant fortitude.

He took gradually to some of the ways of the north. For years he had refused to eat any native food, but now he found that the hot spiced dishes went down very well if washed down by a little Danish Carlsberg or Tuborg lager. It is even said that on his long journeys when he was exhausted in the evening he would mix a little opium with his tobacco to soften the asperities of jungle life and missionary duty. Personally I do not believe this. I think it was one of those mischievous rumours that are started in hot countries and flicker, like some cheating dragonfly, through the bazaars and over the rice fields. However, there is no doubt that Father Ignatius had mellowed. On only one point these days could the full force of his rectitude and unshaken conviction be evoked. He was insistent that his whole flock should receive a full and solemn Christian burial in the rapidly filling but beautifully kept churchyard.

Then, out of the blue, Chow Rart was taken seriously ill with malaria. Dr Wallace was hurriedly recalled from Lampoon some twenty miles away to his bedside. It was no use calling in Bangkok for help. The journey still took six weeks by boat up the Menam Chow Phya and the Mei Ping rivers. But by that time the fever would have long passed, or . . . . Perish the thought. The Mission would be lost without Chow Rart.

But he died. Father Ignatius was distraught. His friend, whom he had so greatly regarded, was dead. It never occurred to Father Ignatius that Chow Rart could be regarded as anything but a Christian. He had adopted their way of life, had attended every service, was one of them, a brown brother in the faith. True, Chow Rart had never actually been converted or formally received into the Church, but his whole life had been a Christian life, not a Buddhist life, so Father Ignatius pressed ahead with one of the best and most elaborate funerals that the north had ever witnessed.

He was surprised when one day, three days before the funeral, the Chow Luang, the Prince, sent for him. Their paths had not crossed often, though they had exchanged civilities on formal occasions – the Prince's birthday, the Songkran festival and at Christmas, which all the Lao people regarded as a fun feast.

Father Ignatius walked slowly up the long drive between its hedges of red hibiscus that he always thought looked wanton and somehow immoral, so unlike the trim flowers of his boyhood in Denmark. He reached the long, low teak house and, as he did so, the door opened and a servant *weid* and led him out into a garden at the rear of the house were the Prince was sitting, dressed in a singlet and a mauve panung, for it was a Thursday.*

Two or three of his children ran off as Father Ignatius approached and the two men were alone. Father Ignatius bowed and the Prince received him with a kindly smile. He spoke in Siamese. 'Please sit down, Father. I have a matter to discuss with you.'

Father Ignatius was glad to be seated under the shade that a traveller's palm gave. They were sitting near a lily pond and the flowers in the morning sun, red, white, yellow and blue, were entrancing and added a touch of cool serenity to the scene.

'I am grieved to hear of the death of my distant cousin, the Chow Rart. A good man.'

*The *wei* is the Siamese salutation made by raising both hands, palm to palm, to his forehead.

Father Ignatius replied, 'Yes, we deeply mourn him. A noble Christian and a dedicated worker....'

The Prince thought for a moment, then said, 'Father, his relatives say he was a Buddhist, always, and they demand he be cremated according to Buddhist custom....'

Father Ignatius kept his composure but his reply was forceful. 'He was one of us, Your Highness. For many years he led a Christian life. He never attended Buddhist ceremonies nor did he pray to Buddha, but to the Christian God.'

The Prince handed Father Ignatius a letter. It was from a son of Chow Rart. It was addressed in terms of deep deference, as was the custom, to the Prince and begged him to ensure that the body of his father was handed over to the family for cremation under Buddhist rites and custom. 'I hand you this letter. It is up to you. I have said that I can take no part in the matter apart from handing you the letter....'

Father Ignatius thanked the Prince and after some polite conversation he took his leave.

Father Ignatius thought the matter over very carefully and then decided to go ahead with the elaborate funeral of Chow Rart, ignoring the request contained in the letter. He just could not let his friend down after all these years during which they had worked together so harmoniously and so well. The funeral went off very well. Hundreds of simple Lao people flocked to pay their last respects but of course the Prince, as was understandable, did not attend, nor did the dead man's family. However, both the British and French Consuls were there with their families and the Tesa, the Governor and representative of the King in Bangkok, came in uniform, officially.

It was a major event in the north and Father Ignatius was as effective and dramatic as ever when he committed the body of his friend to the freshly dug grave.

The matter was forgotten until a new tragedy disturbed the north. Father Ignatius was murdered by Meo tribesmen far from Chiengmai on the Burma border. The tribesmen had been collecting the poppy crop and drying the flowers for opium sale in Rangoon when Father Ignatius stumbled upon them. In a panic they shot him, fearing he was a white policeman from Burma.

Dr Wallace immediately started to make arrangements for his body, which the gang had left behind, to be brought back to Chiengmai. It was over a week's journey by elephant and it is quite certain that, until the procession reached the outskirts of the city, the body of Father Ignatius was carefully strapped to the howdah of the leading elephant. Then, as can happen in Siam, a very strange thing happened. The leading elephant disappeared. The mahout disappeared – and the body of Father Ignatius disappeared too.

It was a complete and baffling mystery. The men in charge of the following elephants in the retinue said that the leading elephant was some way ahead, just out of sight, and when they should have caught up with it, it just was not there . . . .

Chow Rart's successor was a Eurasian known as Jimmy Brown, an agile, dapper little man with the smile of a mischievous monkey. He was very observant. He noticed something and asked to see Dr Wallace. When that busy man could be found he said: 'I think, Sir, that the grave of Chow Rart has been disturbed. It looks as if the flowers have been moved and replaced.'

Dr Wallace went at once to inspect the grave and it was clear that the earth had also just been dug up and very carefully replaced.

With the permission of the Siamese Chief of Police Dr Wallace had the grave and the coffin re-opened.

The body in the coffin was that of Father Ignatius. There was no trace of the body of Chow Rart.

Dr Wallace decided that too many questions arose out of this strange sequence of events. It was clear that Father Ignatius had been killed through his misfortune in surprising a gang of opium growers, who were in no way connected with Chow Rart or his family. Dr Wallace was certain that Chow Rart had now been cremated at Wat Saket, that gleaming temple just along the road. But he would never discover the truth. He could not bear the thought of disturbing the grave again, even if it enabled him to give Father Ignatius the funeral he so richly deserved.

A new priest in charge was appointed to the Mission, a young and enthusiastic man from Liverpool, England. He carried on his work with an energy and dedication equal to that of Father Ignatius. But he was always very careful never to claim a convert unless he was quite sure of his allegiance, and no Christian burial was given to any convert without the consent of his nearest relatives.

It seemed best to play safe.

5

Murder For Love

The very curious and characteristically Edwardian murder case of Hawley Harvey Crippen, the American doctor, who lived at 39 Hilldrop Crescent in North London, will be debated as long as great cases are remembered.

In recent years an increasing body of opinion has inclined to the view that Mrs Crippen, known under her old stage name of Belle Elmore, died from an accidental overdose of hyoscine, or a dose carelessly administered by her husband to keep her asleep so that he could have sexual intercourse in the house with his secretary, Ethel Le Neve, while his wife was unconscious upstairs. I am now one of the minority of criminologists who are convinced that Crippen murdered his wife deliberately for the love of Ethel Le Neve.

In order to understand the extraordinary case of Dr Crippen we must know something of the drug hyoscine. It was a new drug on the market in 1910. It had the effect of decreasing sexual appetite and putting the patient into a deep sleep, far deeper than normal sleep. And, in most cases, the patient on waking could not recollect what had happened in the period leading up to unconsciousness. It was thus a very powerful instrument; for good in specific cases and in the right hands, for evil if administered unscrupulously. Its full properties at this time were realized by few doctors, but Crippen was fully conversant with it.

Although not a very good doctor – he had obtained his doctorate from an obscure American university – he was an expert chemist and his 'practice' consisted largely of promoting and selling new drugs. This was the background to perhaps the most controversial murder case of the century.

Vital, too, to an understanding of the case is a realization of the characters of the three persons involved – Crippen, his wife and his mistress. Dr Crippen might be described as the inoffensive American, at least that was the impression people had of him. He was a mouse-like little man, mild of manner with a sallow complexion and aquiline features. The only remarkable physical feature were his beautiful brown eyes that were gentle and expressive, and a pair of delicate hands with tapering fingers. He was always trying to find the easy way out of the many difficulties that confronted him. Difficulty number one was his wife, who was a monster. Selfish to a degree, vain and extravagant, she was not even faithful. In addition she was often 'indisposed' so that she escaped the housework which she despised. During her indispositions, when she wanted anything and it did not immediately appear, she shrieked at the top of her powerful voice. Her acting career had given her a sense of the dramatic which she used to the full in constant scenes, usually taking the form of abusive rows with her husband, whom she accused of giving her neither enough sex nor enough money.

Ethel Le Neve, Crippen's secretary, was sweet. A charming, shy, gentle person who, unfortunately, fell desperately in love with Crippen. They seemed made for each other and were only happy together. They worked together during the day but at night Ethel had to go back to her lonely lodgings, and Crippen had to return to the noisy, vulgar nagging of his wife. It was a desperate situation.

There was really no way out – unless Mrs Crippen died. Ethel Le Neve had a passion for respectability. She hated being a mistress. She longed to be Crippen's wife. Moreover, she 'felt awful' about Mrs Crippen who was being deceived, for Mrs Crippen had taken quite a fancy to the girl. Her opinion of her husband was so low that it never crossed her mind that Ethel could be deeply in love with him.

Hilldrop Crescent was as respectable as middle-class houses could be at this time and that was still very proper indeed. No one could remember any kind of scandal in Hilldrop Crescent.

It just did not happen. And everyone knew all that went on in every house. In the morning when the gentlemen went to their offices the curtains would gently part and they did so again around seven when the gentlemen returned. All callers during the day were carefully screened by the unseen scrutineers. You could not get away with a thing in Hilldrop Crescent.

So, day after day, Crippen and Ethel played their charade and Mrs Crippen continued to badger and bait her husband, upbraiding him for his lack of worldly success, and his shortcomings as a husband. His shortcomings were becoming manifest, for the more he slept with Ethel the more he hated having to pretend desire for his wife. She sensed this and it made her even more bad-tempered and caused her to flay her husband with a tongue so rasping and bitter that the little man could hardly bear it and survived only by some inner fortitude.

However, not all days were as unhappy as those I have described. Occasionally the Crippens would give a party and Cora – that was another of her names, the one she was christened with – was at her best when they were entertaining old theatrical friends of hers. She loved theatre and circus gossip and because he feared her and was always trying to placate her, Crippen would put his heart and soul into making these occasions a success.

On the last day of January 1910 the Crippens gave one such small dinner party for a married couple and their son, all circus people, and, with a daughter, forming a circus troupe. The evening went off very well, with Cora responding, as she always did, to the stories their visitors had to tell about the great world of entertainment, so garish, so free, so unlike Hilldrop Crescent. Crippen himself had never been in better form. He seemed for an hour or so to have put all his cares aside and he looked years younger. Ethel was not at the party.

Mrs Crippen was never seen alive again by anyone.

Of course, when a wife in Hilldrop Crescent vanished questions were asked. People wanted to know what had happened to her. It was from this moment that Crippen began a series of mistakes that a more experienced liar would certainly have avoided. Cora had gone to visit relatives in California. Well, that was possible. She was an American. There must have been some temptation to get out of London, at least for February and March. And she did have relatives and friends in America. But then Ethel moved into Hilldrop Crescent and tongues really started to wag. Why was Dr Crippen taking his secretary into his house? The answers that were forthcoming were those one would expect. And when the unseen watchers noticed that Ethel was wearing some of the departed woman's rings and necklaces they could hardly contain their disapproval. But this was idle gossip. More dangerous to Crippen were Cora's friends, for Cora had friends. She might be intolerable to her husband but she was a gusty, strong personality and had made a number of friends among her neighbours. They came to offer their sympathy to the grass widower . . . and to have a good look round. One fact astonished them. Cora had left her entire wardrobe behind. So unlike her. She loved clothes and bought more than her husband could afford. Her friends knew how vain she was and they thought she would certainly have wished to dazzle her American cousins with her ' London wardrobe '. They had a point.

Finally the gossip grew in volume and the police heard about it and decided to investigate the disappearance of Belle Elmore or Cora Crippen. An Inspector Drew, who was in charge of the case, took it seriously and made a diligent investigation. He went all over the house with Crippen, missing nothing, creeping into the loft and penetrating the cellar. He even combed the tiny garden and inspected the outhouses. Nothing was found. Inspector Drew was satisfied that for some reason the volatile Cora had bolted. It was not altogether out of character. Maybe Dr Crippen was living with his secretary, but that did not mean that he had murdered his wife.

The file was nearly closed when Inspector Drew called round at Dr Crippen's surgery with one or two routine questions that he thought he should ask and add to the record, though they had little bearing on the case. It was his intention then to close the file. He called expecting to find the doctor and Ethel working away together. He did not find either of them. The owners of the next door shop said: 'They haven't been here for days. Must have gone away. . . .'

That really upset Inspector Drew. Why had they fled? If they had merely gone on a holiday – or a honeymoon – surely some provision would have been made for a locum or at least a notice posted on the surgery to let patients know when Dr Crippen would be back? The inspector decided to go over the house in Hilldrop Crescent again, this time brick by brick.

In the cellar, carefully bricked up and buried in lime, he discovered the body of Cora Crippen.

It was murder – or was it?

Crippen and Ethel should never have fled. They could have gone on living in the Hilldrop Crescent house in adulterous bliss or married harmony. The gossip would have died down and their friends would have supported them. For both had a number of good friends. Ethel was so charming, quiet and gentle. Crippen was known as a kind and courteous man. No one, until now, had had a word to say against him. He was the kind of citizen Hilldrop Crescent respected. Not very successful perhaps, but then, in these Edwardian days, money had not yet become the fetish that it is today. Crippen was very well liked and Ethel was popular.

Why did they bolt? I think they could not bear the house any longer. It had dreadful memories for them both. It was haunted by the savage spirit of Cora Crippen, so that sometimes if Crippen woke at night from a nightmare he would cry out, having heard Cora shrieking at him in her repellent non-stop abuse.

For Ethel too it was a house of ill omen. The house that Cora had dominated, bringing her lover into such misery.

America! If they could only get there together. They would be free of the hideous memories, rid of the nightmares, divorced from the past.

Inspector Drew had the body very carefully removed to the mortuary and then to the laboratory of Dr Spilsbury, the Home Office expert, who was later to be knighted for his services in a distinguished career only to be ended by his suicide. Two grains of hyoscine were found in the decomposing body, which strangely the lime had preserved. It was a massive, killing overdose.

Crippen had purchased five grains of this unusual drug three weeks earlier. The evidence against him was formidable.

The police sent out messages with a description of the couple 'wanted for murder'. Captain Kendall of the SS *Montrose* received the call by wireless. He was bound for Quebec from Antwerp. When he thought about it there was something a little odd about one of the passengers and his somewhat effeminate son. Mr Robinson seemed so devoted to the boy and the boy seemed to be happy only with his father.

The captain suggested to the liner's detective that he take a further look at 'Mr Robinson' and his remarkably silent son who followed him everywhere. The detective was astute and noticed that when Mr Robinson threw an apple to his son, saying catch, the son – who was sitting down – opened 'his' legs. The detective thought this odd. A man would close his legs in these circumstances. Only a woman would open them, making her skirt tight to catch the apple. It looked as if Mr Robinson's boy was a girl in disguise. And so Mr Robinson, who turned out to be Dr Crippen, and his son, who was, of course, Ethel, were arrested and escorted back to England to stand their trial on the charge of wilfully murdering Cora Crippen.

The case against Crippen was very black and the case against Ethel Le Neve was not negligible. Crippen had overwhelming motive, ample opportunity and the corpse had undoubtedly been cut up by him and no one else. He had turned surgeon for the night and completed his grisly task with considerable skill.

But there were questions to be answered. Had Crippen just panicked? Suppose that Cora had died of taking hyoscine given her by Crippen, might she herself have taken the overdose? She was careless with drugs and was apt to drink and take drugs too much. Need Ethel Le Neve have known of the matter in any event? She had motive and possibly opportunity but, on the other hand, was Crippen likely to confide his murderous plan to her?

All the evidence at the long trial at the Old Bailey went to show that Crippen and Ethel Le Neve were deeply and irrevocably attached to each other. Crippen's first thought at all times, and to the end, was to save and protect the woman he loved.

There had, at first, been some difficulty in identifying the corpse, but this was done by those small indications that have, from the beginning of criminal history, caught the murderer. A small piece of surviving skin happened to be just the piece that had the marks of an old stitched scar that Mrs Crippen did in fact have, and Crippen had rather carelessly wrapped the flesh and bones in some old underwear of his own.

The case created the wildest interest, not only in the popular press but in the 'great' dailies, including *The Times*. What everyone wanted to know was: What would the defence consist of? How could Crippen answer the charge against him? Had his lawyers something up their sleeve? In the event the matter followed a curious and unfortunate pattern. Most murderers are cunning, craven little rats who, when cornered, seek only to save their own skins, no matter whom they may hurt or ruin in the process. Crippen was the reverse of this. As soon as he and Ethel had been arrested his one thought was to save her. He seemed regardless and fearless of his own fate.

When he had first slept with Ethel he had enjoyed her, her adoration, and her swift overwhelming response. And he would have been less than human if he had not felt some satisfaction that at last he was able to free his soul and his personality from the bullying possessiveness of Cora. The thought of Cora alone for once, deceived and unable to retaliate, made his affair the sweeter. But this natural male reaction was swiftly followed by love. He found that Ethel meant more to him than anything else in the world. She had brought love and delicacy and excitement into his miserable life. She was his refuge and he loved her with a passion and constancy that matched her own. So his one aim and object, when the blow had fallen, was to make sure, if he could, that Ethel should go free.

Now there was one line of defence that might have enabled Crippen to escape the death penalty. If he had said: 'I gave my wife hyoscine at her request because she suffered greatly from her nerves and, as the drug began to lose its effect for her, she took larger doses. I was appalled when I found her dead and, in panic, I cut up the corpse and hid it . . . .' the jury might have returned a verdict of manslaughter or even of administering a noxious substance It was a credible defence. It would have been impossible to disprove. But Crippen, though advised to plead along these lines, refused to do so. There is no doubt at all that the reason for this was Ethel. She had been in the house with him. How could she not have known? Must she not have been an accomplice? Aiding and abetting him in his ghastly work?

So Crippen put in an impossible plea, that he had never seen his wife after her ' disappearance ' and that he knew nothing of the body under the cellar. This was a blatant lie, but Crippen hoped that at least it would acquit Ethel.

Had Crippen pleaded carelessness, accident, or even suicide, he had a chance of escaping that which most men dread – the rope. He refused to do so and at least two leading ' silks ', including Sir Edward Marshall Hall, who were offered the brief for the defence after the proceedings in the magistrate's court, refused it. They pointed out that Crippen's obdurate and suicidal defence had been deliberately put forward in detail at the police court on Crippen's explicit instructions and that it would be most difficult at the trial to advance a totally different defence, with prosecuting counsel reading out what Crippen had said in his police court evidence and ending up with the question: ' So your evidence so far, Mr Crippen, has been a pack of lies?'

It was not unnatural for leading silks to refuse such a brief, but I would have expected Marshall Hall to accept it. He always had a courage to match that of Crippen, a very brave man. And there were points in Crippen's favour. All the witnesses agreed that he was an honest, hardworking, unselfish, decent person. They liked him. Could such a man become a monster overnight? My answer is that Cora had made her husband just that.

An advocate of the strength of Marshall Hall could have laid his cards on the table and said: ' At the magistrate's court, with the sole object of protecting Ethel Le Neve, Crippen advanced an untenable defence. Now he has decided to tell you what really happened to Cora Crippen and, if you believe his story, which has the ring of truth and is not controverted by any direct evidence, you should acquit him.' This change of plea was well within the range of the great advocate's ability. There was also Erskine's dictum that the advocate has no right to impose his own opinion as to the guilt or innocence of the prisoner between him and the jury's verdict, for this question is one for the jury, not for the advocate. On the acceptance of this principle the whole structure of criminal trials, the whole supposition that a man is innocent until he is proved guilty beyond all reasonable doubt, depends.

In the event, Sir Alfred Tobin defended Crippen more or less along the lines set down by the prisoner, though in his final speech he pointed out that there were other explanations, other possibilities. Ethel Le Neve, however, had the advantage of being defended by Mr F. E. Smith, one of the most able of the younger barristers at the Bar and a future Attorney-General and Lord Chancellor.

I met 'F.E.' only once, when we were both invited to speak at the Cambridge Union in a famous debate. 'F.E.' was, at that time, Secretary of State for India, but he was, of course, a great figure in the Tory Party. Perhaps he was the last of the Tories, which was why Stanley Baldwin, who was a pipe-smoking Edward Heath, disliked him so much. 'F.E.' was not a pale pink. He was a bright and dazzling true blue in politics, and in the court room he was an advocate of great power. His handsome, mahogany face with the jet black hair, the expressive and very large brown eyes, and the voice, clear and incisive, made, with his astounding command both of persuasion and invective, an advocate of great power and attraction.

Sir Alfred Tobin was much liked at the Bar, but no one imagined he was a great advocate. In any case, having accepted the line of defence that Crippen had dictated, his task was, from the beginning, a hopeless one.

When the great trial ended the conviction of Crippen seemed

almost certain. What else could the jury do other than return a verdict of 'Guilty'? Crippen had persisted in a defence which, obviously, consisted of sheer fabrication. The verdict in the case of Ethel Le Neve was in doubt and there were those in court who believed that she would not escape but that she would be convicted as an accomplice.

In the end the verdict was 'Guilty' in the case of Crippen, 'Not Guilty' in the case of Ethel Le Neve. She was freed, married years later, and assumed another name, remaking her life.

Crippen wrote and read out a farewell letter to the world. In it he said: 'In this, my last letter to the public, I say that Ethel Le Neve has loved me as few women love men, and that her innocence of any crime, except that of yielding to the dictates of her heart, is absolute. I give evidence of the absolute innocence of Ethel Le Neve. She put her whole trust in me and what I asked her to do, she did....'

Crippen heard the judge pronounce sentence of death without flinching. For a moment he took Ethel's hand and pressed it in his. It was the last time they ever saw one another. He died bravely, without complaint, leaving a letter for Ethel. But the one vital question now is: must we go along with the theory, more and more the fashionable one, that Crippen did not murder Cora, though she died of an overdose of hyoscine?

My answer to this is that, if Cora died by accident, by her own hand, or even by Crippen's carelessness, it is inconceivable that he would not have called in a doctor and reported the death to the authorities. Finding hyoscine in the stomach had there been a post-mortem – by no means certain – would not have been fatal to Crippen. There were at least three alternative explanations to that of murder and, in view of Crippen's exemplary character and the high regard of those who knew him best, one of these explanations might well have been accepted.

There is surely no explanation of the terrible carving-up of the corpse and the hiding of the body with intent to destroy it, other than terror arising out of an overwhelming sense of guilt.

All the evidence goes to show that Cora was cruel to her

husband in calculated and cunning ways. She used her bitter tongue to make his life a hell. It was not strange that he should decide to still that constant and venomous abuse. As long as Cora was there he had either to take Ethel to seedy cheap hotels, or risk detection in his own house. Cora was quite capable of feigning sleep if she suspected her husband of misconduct. Then his life, already so unbearable, would have become an inferno. Finally, Cora did not trouble to hide her occasional infidelities. She taunted her husband with them when he attempted to assert his own point of view, his own rights in his own house. If ever a woman 'deserved' to be murdered, it was Cora Crippen.

There are women who, unless they are dominated by a man, soon begin to despise him. Cora Crippen was such a woman. She took away Crippen's pride, his honour, his peace and his self-esteem. In the end he took away her life.

The remarkable aspect of the trial of the King against Hawley Harvey Crippen was that the circumstances of the drama showed not only an awful crime, but also a love affair as strong and as true as any that have added a touch of sublimity to a mundane and mercenary world.

6

Never Repeat a Success

Most of the vintage murders of the Edwardian era, like all murders, ended in a trial, at the end of which the jury had to decide, on the facts, whether the accused was 'Guilty' or 'Not Guilty'. The verdict 'Guilty' meant that they were satisfied, beyond all reasonable doubt, that the prisoner had committed the crime as charged. The verdict of 'Not Guilty' might mean either that they thought the accused was innocent or that, although suspicious, they were of the opinion that the evidence fell short of that conclusive certainty 'beyond all reasonable doubt' that the law demands.

This verdict on the facts follows a direction by the judge on the law. The jury have to take these directions on law, but they are not bound to do more than listen to the judge's view of the facts.

No freeman shall be fined or bound
Or disposed of lawful ground
Except by lawful judgment found
And passed upon him by his peers
Forget not, after all these years,
The Charter signed at Runnymede.

Trial by jury has been much attacked lately, but it remains the best possible method of trial. Judges might bring to the task of deciding on facts more expertise, but the jury are of the people, and from the people they receive their mandate.

Although this is the shape of all criminal trials, including murder trials, there are cases in which vital legal questions as to the admissibility of evidence are brought to the attention of the judge by counsel at the beginning of the trial. The jury are then sent out of court, not with the idea of establishing any secrecy but so that the legal points can be argued and a decision taken on what evidence can properly be laid before them. In a few cases the legal decision on this virtually decides the fate of the prisoner. It happens in this way.

Suppose a jury is presented with a case in which a wife has died, apparently by accident, let us say by tripping over some pot plants on a veranda and falling fifteen storeys in a block of flats late in the evening, to the apparent horror of her husband, the verdict will almost certainly be death by misadventure. But supposing it is revealed to the jury that the husband has had two previous wives who have met with a similar tragedy, the jury will tend to assume that the husband had a 'system' for disposing of his nearest and dearest. If to this is added motive, if it appears that in each case the death resulted in a good cash bonus for the husband, the jury's verdict will almost certainly be 'Guilty'.

The question is not as simple as it at first appears. When a man is charged with a crime there is an absolute legal principle that forbids his past (including his previous conviction, if any) being laid before the jury. He is tried strictly on the merits of what he is said to have done in the charge. This is fair and reasonable and is in fact an extension of the basic principle of English law (there is no such thing as 'British' law) that a man is innocent until he is proved guilty.

However, the law is sometimes the master and not the servant of 'principle', and it has long been established that where a 'system' can be proved, as, for instance, where a trickster always adopts the same ingenious method of parting his dupe from his money, evidence of this 'system' can be called. This is justified on the simple ground that if evidence of this nature were excluded then guilty men might go free.

However, the principles we have mentioned have not given up the ghost easily. It is as if they resented being displaced by convenience, even if the convenience or the exception to the general rule was designed solely to ensure that justice should be done. The old entrenched principles fought a battle over the years with the encroachment of evidence as to ' system ', and the result has been that counsel, wishing to call evidence of this character, must show very clearly that indeed there was a system, not just an unhappy coincidence of accidents.

I hope I have not bored you with this simple exposition of the law in this matter. It adds greatly to the interest of Rex *versus* George Joseph Smith, a vintage murder if ever there was one.

The story unfolds itself gently, even decorously, working up to its dreadful climax.

When the trial opened at the Old Bailey, Sir Archibald Bodkin with Travers Humphreys and Cecil Whiteley represented the Crown, while the prisoner was defended by Marshall Hall, who led Montague Shearman and Gratton Bushe.

Before the trial started yet another question arose, and as it involved the whole question of the morality of newspaper purchases of the stories of criminals, or men charged with crime, which has so recently been raised again in the case of Biggs the train robber, let us look into this matter, too, before we unravel the extraordinary story on which the trial of George Joseph Smith was based.

The solicitor instructed by Smith was told by that strange man that he himself had virtually no money, but that he had been approached by a newspaper group who were willing to provide funds to brief the best counsel in London in exchange for his story.

The solicitor was delighted. This meant that they could ' instruct ' a great advocate and he drew up a deed of agreement accordingly and with this in hand employed Marshall Hall.

However, the Home Secretary, Sir John Simon, himself a distinguished lawyer, forbade the deal. He said it was against public policy, unethical, and that no barrister should allow his fees to come from such a source. He also said that the ' Poor Persons ' regulations were designed to cover just these kind of cases.

Marshall Hall was much upset with this prohibition and he wrote a letter to the Home Secretary. As the letter sets out with considerable force and clarity the other side of the dispute I quote it:

3 Temple Gardens

My dear John – I am writing to you direct, as Ernie Blackwell tells me that the letter from the Home Office to Mr Davies, the solicitor, *in re R. v Smith* (Murder), although signed by him, was, in fact your letter. As you have been so recently Attorney-General, and, therefore, custodian of the Bar's honour, I attach much importance to some remarks you make, and regret to say that I am quite unable to understand or accept them. As I understand the facts, they are as follows:

Some time ago, Mr Davies, a solicitor, gave my clerk a retainer for me on behalf of the man Smith, accused of murder. My clerk informed him that the brief would not be accepted unless a very substantial fee was paid with it. This condition was acceded to. Later, the solicitor informed my clerk that the fee required would be forthcoming, as he had made arrangements, on behalf of the accused man, whereby certain people were prepared to provide the funds necessary for his defence.

The brief was not then delivered, but, on the faith of the statement, I consented to have a consultation, and actually to see the accused, which I did. The brief was delivered on Thursday, June 18th (the trial being definitely fixed for June 22nd) and the solicitor then informed my clerk that, as the arrangement for obtaining the money involved the signing of a document by the accused, and the prison authorities had referred the matter to your department, owing to the fact that no reply had been received from you, the fee would not be paid, as arranged, with the brief. My clerk was informed that there would be no delay, and on this assurance, I consented to take the brief, and devoted the whole of Friday, Saturday, and Monday to getting it up. On Monday afternoon, I was personally shown your letter and informed of the further facts.

I understand that the proposal, which you so strongly vetoed, was that the accused should assign to certain named assignees, the copyright of anything he might write for publication, the consideration being the provision of a certain sum of money to be used by the solicitor for the purposes of his defence. I understand further, that this assignment (which your department have and which I have never seen) was, in fact, prepared by counsel (having no connection with counsel for the defence) who had advised that there was no objection to the execution of such a document by the accused.

In spite of your expressed opinion, I regret to say that I cannot see your objection. 'A' charged with murder, and protesting his innocence (and moreover by our law *presumed* to be innocent), has arrayed against him all the resources of the Treasury and the Public Prosecutor, who propose to call some 120 witnesses against him on his trial, which will propably last fourteen days. 'A' has been deprived of all funds in his possession by the action of the police, and he is anxious to be defended. He is told that the particular counsel, whose services he desires to secure, insists on payment of a fee which he cannot provide. An offer is made to 'A' to provide sufficient money for this purpose (note please, nothing for the accused himself) if he will write the history of his life and assign the copyright to the person finding the money. 'A' agrees, but the Home Office authorities decline to allow him to sign the document, and go on to say that the late Attorney-General is of opinion that no counsel at the Bar would accept fees coming from such a source.

For the life of me I cannot follow this, but, as you are such a friend of mine, I feel very strongly the opinion you have formed, and I tell you quite frankly, I was quite prepared to accept fees so provided, and cannot see the objection to my so doing.

If 'A' had been on bail, he could have executed the assignment at his free volition, and the fact that he is detained in custody cannot affect the proposition.

'A' is entitled to be defended by counsel, and counsel are entitled to be paid reasonable fees. In fact, they are not entitled to refuse any brief, if it is for a court in which they practise, and the fee paid is reasonably adequate. This was the opinion given to me by Lord Alverstone and Lord Loreburn, when I consulted them, many years ago, as to refusing a brief which I much wished to refuse at the C.C.C.

Now 'A' is entitled to procure funds for this purpose by any legitimate means, and he can, for this purpose, sell anything that belongs to him which is marketable, e.g. he could execute the necessary conveyance to enable him to sell house property in his possession. Surely he can sell the product of his brain and pen in the same way.

Further, from the counsel's point of view, your experience, fortunately, has not been so long or so sordid as mine, of this class of case. What has sometimes made me feel very unhappy is to know that fees that havc been paid to me for the defence, once the accused has been convicted, have obviously been earmarked as the proceeds, more or less direct, of the crime itself. But the only protection open to a man like myself (who quite against his will has attained a widespread reputation as a defender of prisoners), against being briefed in any important case of the kind that may arise, is to insist that substantial fees should be paid before the brief is delivered. If the solicitor at the last moment is prevented from finding these fees, you say that counsel, in spite of this arrangement, is in honour bound to conduct the case. Although I deny your premisses, I accept your conclusion, and, in spite of every inclination, have consented to represent the accused, and my friend Montague Shearman has adopted the same attitude. Of course, I was not bound to do it, and from every point of view, pecuniary, physical, and professional, I cannot help suffering from being concerned in such a case.

It is too late to alter this now, but I do most strenuously protest that the proposed arrangement (which was being carried out openly in every way, as your letter admits) was in no way against public morality or public interest, and one within the rights of any accused person – of course, there might be conditions attached, which would make such an assignment highly undesirable, or even against public policy, but no such conditions existed in this case.

The letter ends with the friendly signing off of two leaders of the Bar. Sir John acknowledged the letter, but the order stood. The police, on instructions, allowed the small sum found on Smith to be devoted to his fees, but Marshall Hall fought for the life of his client for eleven days for a pittance, giving, of course, much more time to the preparation of the case. Marshall was one of those advocates who literally went into training for big trials, going to bed early, watching his diet and turning away lesser work that might come into his chambers. He always took the view that a murder defence involving the prisoner's life was so supremely important that it outweighed all other considerations, and demanded and deserved the absolute dedication of defending counsel.

The story that Archibald Bodkin unfolded to a jury giving their rapt attention was told in absolute silence, and pressmen there at the time said that the rising tension could almost be felt by public and press alike. The jury seemed transfixed, so absorbed were they.

It was in the month of May that 'Henry Williams', a dealer in antiques, met – and married – Bessie Mundy, the daughter of a former bank manager, who had a private fortune of about £3,000. That may not sound a lot of money in the seventies, but it was a modest fortune sixty years ago. Bessie Mundy had reached the age when she had given up hope of romantic adventure and the sweet, smooth words of Henry Williams completely captivated her. They took a house in Herne Bay. It had no bath but one was quickly installed, quite a small one bought by the faithful Henry. Bessie, of course, in the class-conscious atmosphere of the day, was several tiers above her husband in the social hierarchy, and daughters of bank managers had to have baths in their houses. This bath was small, but long and deep. It was not the type of flat bath or hip bath that servants would bring to one's bedroom in larger houses.

When Henry Williams visited Miss Rapley, the house agent's clerk, he explained, quite gratuitously, that all the money was his wife's. 'I haven't a bean,' he remarked cheerfully.

The next curious event was two visits by Bessie to the doctor. She had had a mild fit, apparently. The doctor could not diagnose anything specifically wrong with her and prescribed a sedative as he thought the excitement of marriage might have been a little too much for her. At the second visit Henry said his wife had had some kind of seizure, but again the doctor could not discover its cause. She was not an epileptic.

Then Bessie made a will leaving everything to Henry. On a Sunday, 13 July, an unlucky day for Bessie, Henry rang the doctor in a highly agitated manner and said that poor Bessie had died in her bath. The doctor hurried round and found this to be true. There were no signs of any violence, no marks on the body. The doctor certified that death had been caused accidentally and the coroner's jury confirmed this by finding a verdict of death by misadventure.

It was the only possible verdict in the circumstances. But it did not satisfy the relatives of Bessie Mundy, for they knew the strange story of the marriage. Henry had had no difficulty in winning Bessie, for she was in the middle thirties and, at this time, that was certainly on the shelf. When Henry came along she thought it was almost too good to be true. It was.

As soon as they were married Henry got hold of a copy of his father-in-law's will and found to his distress that her property was vested in trustees, who paid her the annual income. They were not fools, these people who had been brought up in banks.

However, the trustees had accumulated about two hundred pounds, not yet distributed, and Henry speedily managed to obtain complete control of this sum in cash. He then vanished, leaving his wife to ruminate on the nature of men who appear to be captivated by middle-aged ladies with a secure fortune. That should have been the end of the story, but it was not, for a truly distressing thing had happened. Bessie had fallen in love with Henry and wanted him more and more, dreaming of the day he would return . . . .

The next year it was early spring in Weston-super-Mare, which qualified as one of the most boring little watering places in England. Bessie, who was staying with a school friend, had gone out to buy some daffodils for the house. By the pier, on her way home, she stopped to look out to sea. She was still thinking that one day somehow her prince would return. She turned round and there he was, just the same as ever. He came up to her, saying 'Bessie . . . .' And kissed her.

Bessie should, of course, have sent him away or turned him over to the police, but she did nothing of the kind. Henry was back!

And Henry got busy. He went again very carefully into the question of the £3,000 that was the subject of a trust. Difficult questions of law arose, for the opinion of counsel was taken on the matter. Henry wanted to get full control of all the money without strings. But it appeared that the trustees had full power to purchase an annuity for Bessie and this, of course, would defeat any will she might make leaving the capital to Henry. So Henry decided, to use a vulgarism, that he should get cracking. If a will was presented for probate before the trustees had

had time to act, Henry was home. This, of course, entailed the elimination of Bessie.

Henry got the fortune. Bessie was buried at Herne Bay and the future for Henry seemed comparatively rosy. For three years nothing happened and then, all at once, matters started to move dramatically. A man was arrested in London using the name of John Lloyd. He was neither John Lloyd nor Henry Williams but George Joseph Smith and he was charged with the murder of Bessie Mundy.

How was it that the police felt able to arrest Smith? For the death of Bessie Mundy alone they certainly would not have been able to do so. But delving into Smith's history they dug up two previous wives who had died in the bath in an identical manner. It was too much. They decided to arrest Smith and trust that a trial would lead to his conviction, especially if the court allowed the evidence of the previous deaths to be put in.

It is, I think, worth noting at this point that George Joseph's method of murder was not only legally a 'system'. It was also very systematic. Smith believed in repeating a success. He had discovered that if a woman is lying in a deep and hot bath and you lift her legs swiftly into the air, the blood rushes to the head and she dies within a matter of minutes, losing consciousness in seconds. The body bears no marks. The woman drowns, but in an amazingly brief time.

George Joseph Smith, the antique dealer, had one other expertise and this was it. He could kill a woman more neatly and more swiftly than any man alive. In addition, of course, he had a pervasive sexuality that stunned and ensnared the middle-aged spinsters or widows in whom he specialized. He preferred spinsters. Widows were 'difficult'. It will come as no surprise when I tell you that Mr Smith was married all the time to his childhood sweetheart.

The antique business was an excellent cover. He really did know something about antiques, especially Chinese porcelain. He specialized in '*famille noire*' and '*famille verte*', but was not above buying some '*famille rose*' if the rarer kinds were not available. And he always sold at a profit. So that if curious people wanted to know where he got his money from he could always say that he earned it, that he was a clever dealer and from time to time made a scoop. Oddly the very same gifts that enabled him to win and cheat women were useful in his antique jobbing. He contrived to worm his way into houses, favouring, of course, the houses where lonely women lived. When they parted with 'one or two things' Mr Smith had disparaged them to such an extent that they were glad to be rid of them. He excelled too in the art – still practised in the antique trade today – of 'chatting up' the customer.

Marshall Hall, who was by no means the world's greatest lawyer – and who hated arguing points of law, for he knew his deficiencies, really made a great effort to argue the legal point involved in this case. He argued that no 'system' whatever had been proved, merely a series of strange coincidences. He declared that to allow such evidence would hang the accused before he was tried. He boldly urged that his defence of Smith on the charge of murdering Bessie Mundy would be embarrassed and undermined by the disclosure of evidence of other deaths. He submitted that in this case, as the prosecution was unable to prove that the prisoner had done anything at all of a murderous nature, there was no prima facie case to answer and that, this being so, the admission of other evidence of the nature described simply did not arise. If there was no evidence the case should be dismissed.

It was no good. The judge held the evidence admissible as proving 'system' and from that moment George Joseph Smith was doomed.

Archibald Bodkin was able to put three deaths before the jury.

There was Alice Burnham, whom Smith had married, who had left him all she had – and who had died in her bath.

Margaret Elizabeth Lloyd, whom Smith had married, who had left him all she had – and who had died in her bath.

And now there was poor Bessie Mundy, whom Smith had married, who had left him all she had – and who had died in her bath.

With these facts, which he was allowed to open to the jury,

Archibald Bodkin was able to make a dreadful and effective speech. It seemed that the man in the dock was indeed a monster who preyed on middle-aged spinsters for their money.

Even so, had Smith's character, as it came out in the trial, contradicted this monstrous catalogue of crime, he might have a chance. Unfortunately he came across as mean, cunning, deceitful and an insolent hypocrite. If little things mean a lot the jury could not help forming a very poor view of George Joseph Smith.

He gave his wife a 'pauper's' funeral. This was the cheapest and most humiliating way of disposing of the dead. Unfortunately the Church accepted that if you died poor you did not deserve a decent funeral. Christ, had he lived in Edwardian times, would certainly have been buried in this way had he not been sent to a criminal lunatic asylum. But George Joseph's explanation for giving his wife this mean and degrading farewell was typical of the man. 'After all, when they're dead, they're dead,' he said. How true.

Smith was mean of mind as well as incredibly mean with the money he made out of murder. When the father of Alice Burnham thought it wise to find out rather more about the man his daughter wished to marry, he wrote to Smith asking a few questions about his background. This was a perfectly normal letter to write, certainly at this time. Parents still felt they had some responsibility for children's marriages, especially for the daughters. The marriage settlement was still in vogue. And fathers still expected young men who wished to marry a daughter of the house to turn up, impeccably dressed, and to ask for permission to marry the girl of their choice.

This permission was by no means always granted. But when it was, there was often a period of waiting which the parents thought wise in case the young people had been too impetuous. This system paid handsome dividends in keeping the divorce rate at a very low level. A father felt he had to make sure of the kind of man his daughter was seeking to marry. After all, if anything went wrong, if he left her for other women or for another woman, according to the cruel custom of the day society, at all levels, would say: 'It serves her right. Any woman can keep a man if she tries hard enough.'

In view of all this one would have thought that young Mr Smith would have replied respectfully, if not graciously. The reply he did send read as follows:

Sir – In answer to your application regarding my parentage, my mother was a Bus-horse, my father a cab-driver, my sister a rough-rider over the Arctic Regions. My brothers were all gallant sailors on a steam-roller. This is the only information I can give to those who are not entitled to ask such questions contained in the letter I received on the 24th inst.

Your despised son-in-law,
G. Smith.

There is no doubt at all that Smith had some kind of fascination, perhaps a mesmeric power, that completely subdued middle-aged women. When he put himself out to please them they did not have a chance. They were as good as dead. The time between the marriage and the murder was only the time required to transfer their whole fortune to their husband. Smith used a new name for each murder. He specialized in women who had a little social background: a bank manager's daughter, a clergyman's daughter, and the daughter of a retired builder. He shunned alike the upper class – right out of his line of business – and the working class, much too earthy and shrewd and, of course, too poor. The day of the wealthy, lazy artisan had not yet arrived.

In choosing his victims as he did Smith knew that he was playing his deadly game on the right terms. These women were not drab nonentities. Smith had a most engaging manner when he chose to use it, and in the antique business he occasionally was given the entrée to some great house whose owner wished perhaps to dispose of some silver or china discreetly. This enabled Smith to do quite a bit of name-dropping, and this was very effective with his widows and spinsters. A man who could speak of a baronet by his first name and was obviously familiar with his 'seat' could not be a ruffian. Simple snobbery pervaded the Edwardian scene. It was not the snobbery of money or intellect. It was the simple snobbery of those who dearly loved a lord.

The trial itself, before Mr Justice Shearman, was, to say the least, eventful. At first Smith remained calm, even when the prosecution produced the three baths in court – the murder baths – but when the police were called to give their evidence Smith raved against them and the judge was unable to stop his obscene tirades.

Smith had apparently only loved one woman, a Miss Pegler, and she came to court to give evidence. She said that, on the whole, he had been kind to her. This was something in Smith's favour, but she spoilt it all by adding that Smith had warned her about baths. 'Very dangerous for women,' he said, 'they can faint and drown in them.' An odd remark. Fainting, of course, was, at this time, a female pastime. Not to faint on occasion was considered unfeminine. So a warning about women fainting did not then sound ridiculous, as it might today.

But how did the women die? There was really no doubt that Smith had murdered them, but how? The police carried out an experiment. They asked a girl, strong and athletic, to get into a warm bath and to allow them suddenly to raise her legs high in the air. As her head sank she at once became unconscious. They had difficulty in reviving her. The evidence of Sir Bernard Spilsbury, the famous Home Office pathologist, was vital on this point. He gave evidence that when water suddenly entered the mouth, ears and nose they might die of shock before drowning. But it was still 'might'. There was still a loophole that had not been closed.

The jury, however, had been tremendously impressed by the police experiment and shocked by the arrogant raving of the man in the dock.

The prosecution case ended. Marshall Hall rose and said: 'I call no evidence.' This was a way of saying: 'There is no case to answer.' But there was a case to answer and as he now had the right to the last word he attempted to answer it in detail and at large. It all amounted to this: 'None of us know how these women met their death. None of us know that the prisoner murdered them. It is all surmise, not that proof beyond all reasonable doubt that the law demands.'

Mr Justice Shearman summed up against the prisoner in a way that would not be tolerated today. He even gave a new and dramatic display of how the dead women might have met their end. Perhaps Smith had carried his brides into the bath and then raised their knees with his left arm, while pushing their head down and immersing it with his right hand. There was no evidence of this at all, but so impressive was the judicial charade that several members of the Bar attributed the verdict to this extraordinary demonstration.

There was, of course, an appeal, but it failed both on the point of admissibility of evidence we discussed at the beginning of the chapter, and on the point of misdirection by the judge.

The police had a far more extensive dossier on Smith than was used at the trial. He had swindled several women whom it was not necessary for him to murder.

They were fortunate. They only lost all the money they had.

George Joseph Smith had a macabre sense of humour. After murdering 'Mrs Lloyd', his landlady heard this satanic man playing the piano in the sitting-room.

He was playing 'Nearer my God to Thee'.

7
Unsolved

The majority of murder cases follow the pattern one would expect. A victim dies, done to death, suspicion falls on a man or woman who is arrested. There is an inquest, police court proceedings, and, eventually, a trial. This leads to the full evidence both for the prosecution and for the defence being heard, perhaps for the first time, and the matter concludes with the judge's summing-up and the verdict.

While all this is going on the case is *sub judice* and it is a firm rule of law that comment by the press or by the government is not allowed until not only the trial is concluded but any appeal is also finalized.

The world was shocked by President Nixon's announcement that appeared to condemn the Sharon Tate accused while they were being tried for murder. The fact that people suspected of and charged with murder are hippies, or drug fiends, or religiously perverted, does not mean that they should be denied a fair trial. It is, in fact, from the point of view of public morality more important that they should be seen to receive a completely fair trial without the prejudice their activities may provoke. It is lunacy for a head of state to make his private views known during a trial in which the lives of the accused are at stake.

The administration of the law has, from time to time, to carry on a war against public prejudice directed towards an individual or a group of persons. Sometimes the venue of the trial is changed if there is any possibility of local prejudice preventing a fair trial. But what of prejudice and secret whisperings that pursue a person involved in a murder case but never charged for lack of evidence? This presents a ghastly dilemma for the man or woman concerned. There is no way in which he or she can obtain a public clearance and certificate of character. People may still say: 'He was lucky. He did it, but they could not prove it.' In Scotland, of course, the verdict of 'Not-Proven' and the verdict of 'Not Guilty' distinguish between the innocent and the suspected who cannot be convicted, but suppose you are never charged? Then you cannot be cleared of a stigma the public may brand you with. You cannot ask to be charged in order to clear your name. It is an awful predicament and in a few cases has led to tragedy.

I choose the case of Major General Luard and his wife, for they were both the last people in the world whose lives one would expect to be smashed by murder, robbery, shooting and suspicion and suicide.

In the long hot summer of 1908, in the month of August, families like the Luards seemed as secure and as happy as it was possible to be. Military pensions were not generous but, so cheap was living at this time, they were adequate, and the Luards, as so often was the case in the Services and the professional classes, had modest means of their own to supplement the general's pension. Charles Edward Luard was seventy. His wife, Caroline, was nearly sixty. They lived at Ightham Knoll near Sevenoaks. Apart from one great house in the neighbourhood the country population included many retired Service people and this made life for the general and his wife more congenial. They had friends and acquaintances and were very well liked.

The general still played golf with a handicap of fourteen. The Godden Green Golf Club was just under three miles from their front door. The general was wont to walk to the golf course. He thought nothing of it. Besides, more often than not some car-owning friend would give him a lift. The general took the *Morning Post*, one of the best newspapers ever published in England, and his views on affairs were predictably Tory. He believed in the Empire, the British world mission, the Raj in India, where he had spent part of his service, good manners (especially to one's 'inferiors'), good claret, sportsmanship, and the code by which he and his wife and 'people like ourselves' lived.

This code insisted that marriage was a life-long partnership sustained by love. Sex and money were not topics of conversation. They could be debated privately, but not with one's friends. The general, of course, was devoted to the monarchy and in a small room at the back of the house he had his orders and medals on display. These included the Companion of the Bath, the Order of St Michael and St George, and a large number of medals arising out of campaigns in South Africa, the Sudan and India. He also treasured the Distinguished Service Order. He was wont to say: 'When it comes down to it, and the politicians have got us into a mess, it's the soldier they call in to put things right.'

Their habits were not identical with English habits today. The general smoked a pipe. His wife, of course, did not smoke. They had a 'proper' breakfast – kippers, eggs and bacon, fruit and coffee. They dined at night by candlelight waited on by one of their two maids. They had a cook but no gardener. Caroline Luard did the garden. They did not run a car. Very few people had yet bought the new locomotion. They subscribed to the local hunt though they did not ride to hounds. This meant that in the winter they would attend the meets if they were not too far away, and meet their friends.

Very occasionally they would give a dinner party for six guests. The time on the invitation was 8 pm. At eight precisely all the guests arrived. It was considered extremely bad form to be even ten minutes late – or early. The general on these occasions really enjoyed himself. The friends invited, apart from the rector, who was always included, would certainly help to bring back earlier days, pig-sticking in India (the general had once won the Kadir Cup) and days when he and Caroline had first seen Malta, Port Said, Aden, Bombay, Penang and those other treasured and very British places between London and Hong Kong.

If, from this description of the Luards, you think that they were conventional and narrow-minded, this was not so. Charles

Luard had seen much too much of life to wear blinkers. He knew and recognized tyranny when he saw it, deceit, corruption, treason and double-dealing. He was completely honest in all his dealings and he was tolerant of the idiosyncrasies of his friends and of the world at large. Of course he had his prejudices. He thought that the British soldier was the best in the world, though he had a healthy respect for the German Army. He expected people to have good manners. He had gone to school at Winchester and urbanity and a calm approach were second nature to him. Among the things he liked were Harris tweed, women, especially his wife, friends, the countryside, biographical books, golf and crumpets for tea. Objects of his dislike or disapproval included Burgundy, gin, cocktails, 'intellectuals' ('the brittle intellectual who cracks beneath the strain'), upstarts and overt immorality.

People like the Luards may seem out of this world today but in 1908 they were very much part of the pattern of English life. By the way, the word 'English' was still normally used to describe the inhabitants of England. The Scots, the Irish and the Welsh were admittedly not quite English but the best of them tried to be English and the word 'British' was used mainly to describe British subjects, including the two hundred million British subjects in India who owed allegiance to His Majesty, the King Emperor, in London. There was very little cant about the Luards and their friends. They were not hypocrites. They were absolutely sure of their values and 'priorities', though they would not have used that bastardized term. They believed, it is true, in keeping up appearances, but they did not believe in keeping up with the Joneses. They went to church each Sunday, always occupying the same pew immediately behind the curtained pew of the great house, for two reasons: Caroline Luard was naturally devout and the general looked upon God as his commanding officer. They also genuinely believed that they had the duty of setting an example to those in society not so fortunate as themselves.

Perhaps you now have in your mind's eye the kind of people that Charles and Caroline Luard were. Today it is fashionable to deride the faith and attitudes I have described, but as I knew many people like the Luards, as a boy and young man, I must say I still admire them. They were kindly, honest, often amusing, without snobbery, without cant or pretence, without meanness, loyal to their friends, their ideals and, of course, to their country. When tragedy struck it seemed all the more outrageous and horrible. On a Saturday in mid-August, a lovely warm day when the countryside was at its best and most benign, Charles and Caroline Luard left their house together. He was going to collect his golf clubs as they had been asked to stay the weekend with friends. Caroline Luard was going to the 'Casa', which was a deserted bungalow surrounded by bracken and trees where she often went to pick flowers or read. They parted and the general later was offered a lift on his return from the links by the padre, but he refused, saying he liked the walk. Both Caroline and Charles walked a lot. It kept them exceptionally fit for their age. The general met a Mrs Stuart, who was calling on Caroline. He asked her in, giving her tea, China tea served in some porcelain that Caroline had inherited from her mother.

The general said: 'Caroline is late. I wonder what's happened to her?' But he was not worried. However he did walk over to the Casa after Mrs Stuart had left.

He found his wife on the veranda lying head downwards on the floor with two bullet wounds that had shattered her skull and blown out her eyes. Four valuable rings had been taken from her fingers. Later it was confirmed that the rings had been removed after her death.

The general was overwhelmed and distraught. He had to face two inquests. He sold his house and went to live with a Mr Ward who was a member of parliament and a friend. But suspicion followed him everywhere.

On what was that suspicion founded?

The general did not have an absolute alibi at the golf club. He just could have gone to the Casa *en route*. The general had firearms in his house that could have been used in the killing. There was some evidence that he was quick-tempered when roused.

This, of course, did not amount to anything like proof that he had murdered his wife. He had perhaps opportunity, but there was no motive. No one found the rings. None of the firearms at the house had been used that day. His manner at the golf club, when he met the parson *en route*, and when he asked Mrs Stuart in to tea, was as calm, as assured and as genial as he habitually was. He would have had to be a consummate actor to have given this impression if, in fact, he had just committed a brutal murder.

On the face of it it seemed to be robbery with murder by an unknown man. But the public began to whisper and continued to whisper. No robber had been identified. No robber had been caught. The general was there and he had to bear a campaign of secret calumny that was as vicious as it was uncorroborated by any known facts.

What is it that makes members of the public indulge in a witch hunt from time to time? I suppose it is an old primeval instinct. One member of the pack is in difficulties and, as one, the pack turns on him and rends him to bits. I think that this kind of thing was more apt to happen in the Edwardian age than it is now, when we all see so many sides to any given question. However this may be, happen it did and the poison pen writers got busy having a field day, slipping little notes under the general's door when he was out, or sending them through the penny post.

The fact that there were two inquests made matters much worse for Charles Luard. The whole facts were thrashed out twice and new witnesses were introduced who had seen red-haired ruffians and seedy old tramps in the neighbourhood of the Casa about the time when it appeared that Caroline Luard was being shot at close range by a murderer whom she must have seen coming towards her.

At the end of the day the net result was that it was proved that Caroline Luard had been murdered and that her rings had vanished, taken from her fingers after death. They were valuable early Victorian rings set in gold or pinchbeck. One was of diamonds, a central stone with two satellites. One was a sapphire and diamond ring, while the third was a large opal of good quality which she often wore, refusing to believe the myth about opals being unlucky. The rings – like the china – had come from her mother and Caroline Luard wore them all the time. The rim marks were still on her fingers when her husband found her.

The time of the murder was fixed fairly exactly at 3.15 by two reliable witnesses who had heard shots at that time. Where was Charles Luard at 3.15? Well, he was at the Godden Green Golf Club at 3.30 and he could not have walked the distance in fifteen minutes. He was seen walking to the club at 3.25 at least twenty minutes' walk from the Casa. So, if this evidence was accurate, he could not have murdered his wife.

But it was the general who had found her. And the times were approximate. There were still a lot of suspicious people who believed that the general had killed his wife and then proceeded to set up a convincing alibi.

There was no evidence at all that Caroline Luard was meeting a lover at the Casa and, at her age, it was most improbable. There was no evidence that the Luards had had violent or bitter quarrels either on the day of the murder or before. All the evidence went to show that they were happily married.

Yet the coroner's verdict that Caroline Luard had been shot to death by a person or persons unknown did nothing to free the general from the awful accusing finger of suspicion that was still being pointed towards him by people who were judging the matter, not from the facts, but from supposition. 'Well, somebody killed her. The coroner found that she had been murdered. And no one else was ever identified.' This was the argument, impossible to answer, for it rested not on fact or proof, but on prejudice.

The Luard servants went into the box to say that their master and mistress were a devoted couple. And, giving evidence at the inquest, Charles Luard seemed overcome with grief, a completely shattered man.

What really happened?

There has been a certain amount of speculation that Mrs Luard was murdered by a man named Dickman, who two years later was convicted of a train murder. Dickman was executed for this murder. Dickman is supposed to have forged one of Caroline Luard's cheques, and met her and murdered and robbed her in an arranged meeting. There is really no evidence of this, though the theory has been mentioned by writers on unsolved murders when they are attempting to lift the veil that still shrouds the Luard case.

Although there is no factual evidence, it must be said that the murder of Caroline Luard bore all the marks of a brutal crime committed for gain by a brutal criminal. It bore none of the marks that characterize domestic murder, the killing of a wife by an outraged or insane husband.

The police put in an immense amount of work on the Luard case and got nowhere. They had no evidence to arrest anyone. If Caroline Luard was killed at 3.15 the murderer could have caught the 3.45 to London and lost himself in the great city. The general did not reach the scene till before 6.0, by which time the Sevenoaks train would have decanted its passengers and the murderer would have made good his escape. This is a plausible theory. It does not go against what we know of the shooting or of the people involved. It is, on the face of it, extremely unlikely that Charles Luard if he was sane – and he had always been regarded as a quiet, balanced man with a sense of humour – should suddenly become a man who could slaughter his own wife and then set up an alibi giving the most convincing performance of utter bewilderment and grief. It is almost unbelievable that this man could have become so evil overnight. As the late Lord Birkenhead once remarked in another famous murder case: 'People do not suddenly become evil.'

Now the secret of this terrible crime will never be known. Dickman, thought by some to be the murderer, was executed for another crime. The friends of Charles and Caroline Luard maintained an absolute conviction that the general was completely innocent. But what a relief it would have been if the police had pursued the matter to success and tracked the murderer down. Then and only then would the evil gossip have been stilled for ever.

As it was Charles Luard never recovered from his wife's death. The tragedy finished him as a man. Soon after going to live with his friend John Ward he went for a walk one day and threw himself in front of a local train. He was killed instantly. He left a note saying that he had gone to join the wife he loved. 'Something has snapped. I can bear it no longer.'

Charles Luard, a good man and a fine servant of his country, had been murdered himself by malicious gossip that hounded him to his death.

The coroner's verdict found that he had taken his own life while the balance of his mind was disturbed.

8
Mr Hassan

Do you know Beirut? Oh, but you should. In normal times, when it is not dragged reluctantly into the boiling politics of the Near and Middle East, it is the most delightful and westernized of Near Eastern cities. Beirut has everything. Here, at the St George's Hotel on the waterfront, the foreign correspondents are crowding the bar because it is so much pleasanter to report the news from Egypt, Algeria, Iraq or Syria from this sophisticated little capital with its hundred night clubs where you can buy anything at all. Then the Lebanese, in normal times, are so charming. Half-Christian, half-Arab, the population is agreed on the pursuit of money. And the Lebanese are real experts in the field of finance, insurance, banking and the allied skills. There are some very rich men in Beirut. Of course, there are poor men too, but one does not see them for they live very quietly in shanty towns on the outskirts of the city. As a rule the gay hubbub of Beirut is not troubled by the poor. It is too dazzled by the rich.

There is one English-language paper as well as a French-language paper and, of course, several Arab newspapers whose great scrawled headlines – from right to left – in green and red look, to the ignorant European, as if some giant dragonfly had left his mad pigmentation across the page. The English-language paper has a very lively young lady columnist and she sets the tone of busy, speculative Beirut – daily:

Lingering over a vodka and lemon in Le Vendôme who should I see but Harry Inchcape – recently divorced from his artist wife Suzy – who told me that he had just looked in to see his old friends the Abu Izzidines on his way to Cannes where he relaxes for a fortnight. With him was a stunningly beautiful girl, Jeanne Le Patrick, who, I understand, models. Good to see Harry again, looking no more than his fifty-eight years.

This evening to the poker and kiss party given by Sandy McDougall and his wife Estelle at their down-town villa, the Nightingale. Sandy has recently taken over as Second Secretary at the Canadian Embassy, from the Ronnie Braithwaites who have flown to Moscow for Ronnie's new posting....

And so on and on and on.

You get the atmosphere? Rich, rare, down-to-earth, right up-to-date. Nothing about the future of the Lebanon. Nothing about the Arab cause. Nothing to annoy the Israelis – or anyone else. Just well-informed gossip to make the in-folk feel at home.

I said Beirut has everything and this is true. The country is only some eighty miles long by fifty wide, so that you can see it all in a couple of days, but it will have given you fantastic changes. One hour from the 85° heat of summer Beirut you can motor into the Cedars of Lebanon and ski on some of the best snow slopes in the world. Back at night to gamble by a warm and shimmering sea at the casino with the largest – and most lovely – girl revue in the world. Oh, yes. Beirut has everything. Long may she endure. She has been called the happy harlot. It is quite unfair. Beirut just plays the western game the winning way. And if you thought this was the real Lebanon you would be much mistaken, for under the smooth western façade the life of the Arabs goes on and, just occasionally, the strong currents of that real life, founded on fifteen hundred years of Moslem tradition, break surface to stun the complacency of Beirut society.

In 1906 the life of the Arab population was not hidden from the casual visitor by a modern international façade, not even by a French overlordship. The rule of His Imperial Majesty, the Sultan of Turkey, still reached out as far as Egypt. It was a great empire and it united Islam under one despotic, if benevolent, emperor.

But the position of the Lebanon in the decade before the First World War was a curious one. The Porte had ultimate control but the European powers, especially the French, were deeply interested in the country, and influential as well. The large Christian population was used as a justification for interference and a semi-autonomous status was granted to the ' district ', with the reluctant concurrence of the Porte.

In this period the pattern of Lebanon today started to develop. Money came in from Lebanese who had emigrated to Africa and other parts where the Lebanese businessmen made rings round the local establishment. The first tourists penetrated the Lebanon and eccentric Englishwomen, like Lady Hester Stanhope, settled in or near Beirut with their large Arab houses, their night and day gardens and their African slaves. In this period, too, the first stirrings of modern Lebanese nationalism, which were later to be subdued by a long French occupation, started to reveal themselves. The Europeans were arrogant. The Turks were often insolent and overbearing. The Arabs suffered, but they did not suffer gladly and just occasionally their anger would erupt.

Lebanon had always attracted those who sought an entirely different way of life, and a hundred years before the incident of Mr Hassan, Lady Hester Stanhope had settled near Sidon in the modern Lebanon, though this was then regarded as being part of Syria. As her sojourn has some bearing on our story I quote Dr Meryon's account of this fantastic woman.

In 1810, impelled by a strange belief in her destiny, she left England, and after wandering restlessly for a year or two on the shores of the Mediterranean, she repaired to Syria and finally settled in 1813 at the deserted convent of Mar Elias, beside the little village of Jun and within 8 miles of Sidon. Here, wearing the dress of an emir – weapons, pipe and all – she ruled her Albanian guards and her servants with absolute authority. The old convent, perched upon an isolated eminence among the wildest scenery of the Lebanon, was soon converted into a fortress garrisoned by Albanians, and it became a refuge to all the persecuted and distressed who sought her assistance. So powerful was the influence which she wielded over the surrounding country, that Ibrahim Pasha, when about to invade Syria in 1832, was constrained to solicit her neutrality. After the siege of Acre in the same year, she is said to have sheltered several hundred refugees. She adopted, along with the garb of a Mohammedan chieftain, a good deal of the Mohammedan religion, and her faith seems to have been based both upon the Koran and the Bible. She practised astrology and other secret arts, and always kept in a magnificent stable two mares, on which she fancied she was to ride into Jerusalem with the Messiah at his next coming. During the latter years of her life, when her profuse liberality had loaded her with debt, she was compelled to submit to many humiliations, and she died 23rd June, 1839, with no European near, surrounded by a crowd of servants who plundered the house of everything that could be stolen the moment that the breath had left her body. She was buried in the garden adjoining her residence.

Lady Hester was not forgotten and her legend lived on, with the result that a hundred years later, in 1906, there were a large number of Americans and British living a Moslem life in the Lebanon, having broken away from the restricting and inhibiting atmosphere of Washington, Baltimore, Liverpool or London. One such man was Wilbur Dangerfield, who was a Bostonian, with all that that implies.

It has never been made clear what it was that made Wilbur Dangerfield walk out of a secure and well-heeled life in Boston to seek adventure in the Lebanon. After his wife died in a train accident he felt lonely. His work as vice-president of a local bank failed any longer to excite or even interest him, and his son and two daughters were grown-up and away in New York. Certainly an account he read of Lady Hester may have had something to do with it. What a woman! What a life! The life of a pasha, an emir, a sultan, king of all he surveyed. He left the bulk of his fortune beautifully invested in the States, taking a mere quarter of a million dollars with him. After a long journey by ship to Italy and then to Beirut he looked for a suitable castle or even a vacated monastery which he might make into a home. He decided that he would enter the life of the people absolutely as Hester had done. And with this in mind he read everything he could lay his hands on that shed light on the Arabs, their habits, language, tradition, literature and above all their faith.

If he was to do the thing properly he saw very early on that to be a Moslem would make him cease to be a foreigner, an outsider. It was not the colour of their skin that bound these people together, but their religion. Their religion was a way of life, not merely a faith, and the whole pattern of their days from morning till night was governed by the Koran. Wilbur studied the Koran and the life of Mohammed in English translation.

He was tremendously impressed. This dynamic revolutionary who, fifteen centuries ago, had banished the idols and the idolatry, introducing the amazing pattern of all men equal before one god, this was a truly fabulous story.

He settled in a fortress near Tyre. It had been used by a French commander after its evacuation by the Turkish garrison, but the Turks returned and built new buildings for their army. They were delighted to sell to the mad American the fortress on a promontory that ran into the sea. It was a wild and desolate place but, with systematic thoroughness, Wilbur made it into quite a grand home. It had a castellated outer wall, turrets, a moat and a drawbridge. It had twenty-five rooms and a banqueting hall and there were eleven Arabs who seemed attached to the place much as cats will attach themselves to a building. Ten of the eleven were obviously hangers-on, servants who hoped to go with the fortress, but one man was different. Mr Hassan was a magnificent-looking specimen of manhood, fair – for his mother had been Turkish – and commanding. His eyes were grey and his beard stained crimson. He wore a gold dagger hanging from the belt of his robes. As soon as Wilbur had settled in, Hassan made it clear that he was Wilbur's bodyguard and number one retainer. He stood there, making that ancient Turkish salutation that starts at the forehead and travels down with a bow that denotes homage. Wilbur found this irresistible. He took Mr Hassan on.

The household were all Moslem except Wilbur himself. The Christians kept to themselves and there was no love lost between the Christian Arabs and the Moslem Arabs, so residents from abroad – and there were at that time very few of them – were, in fact, compelled to choose to run either a Moslem or a

Christian household. To have had a mixed ménage would have invited chaos, if not bloodshed.

Moslem and Christian were not the only dividing lines in the Lebanon. The Druses, powerful and influential, were heterodox Moslems and so were on very bad terms with the main Moslem community. The Maronites, too, were very independent, having their own bishops, and it took an outsider years to appreciate the many subtle hatreds that kept the pot boiling in the land that stretched from the mountainous Cedars of Lebanon to the sea.

The only stabilizing factor were the Turks. Although they allowed the local emirs considerable freedom to rule their own people, it was the Turkish governors and commanders who represented supreme power. Their ancient empire, comprising most of the Moslem world, had been much criticized as being autocratic and even despotic. But it was also benevolent, not unlike the British Raj in India, except that the Turks were much less keen on 'progress' than the British and had no illusions about democracy or home rule.

There was really only one major crime in the Ottoman Empire and that was treason. This was very widely interpreted. Any political demonstration, and subversive organizations were included in this term, was treason, and those who were caught were immediately hanged at dawn in the square of their home town. So that was that. It was better not to play politics in the Sultan's domains. Apart from this there was much freedom. There was virtually no education. All the windows on the world were shut but a man was free – unless he was a slave – to hire his labour, to trade, to make and save money. There was considerable security and there was peace. Of course, once a year the governors had to provide a strong levy of young men for the Turkish Army, the recruits serving, as a rule, for two years. And the emirs themselves had to travel to the Porte at least once in three years to make their homage and swear their allegiance to the Lord of Life. But apart from this the ordinary citizen was not harassed by the government. Even in the matter of religion there was much freedom and the Christians at the time we are speaking of were not persecuted. They had to watch their step so that they did not infringe the law of the Koran, but, provided they were careful, they were left alone.

Wilbur Dangerfield had brought no companion with him from Boston but he soon decided to take a native girl as his companion. She was the daughter of a very good family who claimed descent from the Prince Fakh Ad-Din, famous in sixteenth-century Lebanese history. Wilbur called her ' Martha ' and she called him ' My Lord ', which suited Wilbur fine.

Martha helped Wilbur in his study of the Moslem story and the Moslem faith. She managed to borrow some books on the subject for him and would read to him in the evenings. She read English well and Wilbur realized that he was exceptionally lucky to have attracted a girl who was both handsome and could speak his own tongue. After six months Wilbur suggested marriage but Martha said: ' Wait till you become a Moslem, my master.'

So Martha read the history of the Prophet Mohammed and his new astounding code of life to Wilbur. He listened entranced to Martha as she read to him of the early life of Mohammed, his success as a merchant and a diplomat, his marriage to Khadijah and the visions that came to him in middle age, visions of such brilliance and clarity that they changed his life and created a new religion that was to give over a hundred million people a way of life and a firm belief in Paradise.

He made it a practice to spend a certain portion of each year in a cave on Mount Hira, and here, when he had reached his fortieth year, he had a vision, in which he received a message from God through Gabriel, which is found at the beginning of the ninety-sixth sura of the Koran. This vision is said to have caused him much distress of mind, and he returned to Khadijah with a fear that he had become possessed, and by her he was soothed and comforted, and encouraged to await fresh visions. After a period of much anxiety and excitement, fresh visions came, and he felt that he had been called to become a prophet of God, and was entrusted with a mission to bring a pure religion to the world. Of his sincerity at this period there is absolutely no reason to doubt. Prolonged meditation and asceticism have in all ages of the world been fruitful in visions and dreams, while Mohammed was rendered peculiarly liable to such hallucinations by the circumstance that from his childhood he had suffered from a nervous disease which by modern physicians has been considered to have been either epilepsy, catalepsy or hysteria. He found the first believer in his claims in his wife Khadijah, and his love for her in consequence grew to such a height of affectionate reverence that after her death he placed her among the only four perfect women the world ever saw. His next converts were the inmates of his household, his slave Zaid, and his most intimate friend Abu Bekr, a man of great probity and prudence, who possessed considerable influence in Mecca. The last won for him several more converts and soon a little community was formed, the members of which united in the practice of prayer and the acceptance of the messages through Mohammed. The progress of the new sect, however, was very slow at the outset and in the first three years it secured only fourteen proselytes, and an attempt made by Mohammed to gain the support of the Hashimites, the family to which he belonged, procured for him only the adherence of his cousin Ali, a lad of sixteen, the remainder being moved only to ridicule. But the matter had now become public, and Mohammed, undaunted by his failure, began to preach openly to his townsmen his new revelations. His first appeals were directed against the folly of idolatry, and in favour of the recognition of the one all supreme God, who required of man submission and loyal obedience, but the irreligious Meccans, who set him down to be an enthusiast, a poet, or simply a man possessed, replied to his fervent appeals with sarcasm, mockery and open ridicule. In reply Mohammed reminded them of the way in which former prophets had been received, threatened them with destruction in this life and terrible punishment in the next, and meeting taunt with taunt he ridiculed the idols of the Kaaba in the most outspoken manner. As they did not believe in him, they only laughed at his threats; but his attacks upon idolatry threatened their self-interest, and as they derived much profit from their position as guardians of the Kaaba, they waited upon Abu Talib, Mohammed's guardian and the head of the family, and urged him either to impose silence upon his nephew or to withdraw his protection. This Abu Talib refused to do, but he sent for Mohammed privately, told him what had passed, and urged him for the sake of the family to desist. This appeal, coming from one who had so long befriended him, was harder to resist than the hostility or scorn of strangers, but Mohammed replied, 'Though they gave me the sun in my right hand and the moon in my left to bring me back from my undertaking, yet would I not pause', and then burst into tears and turned to leave. On this the good Abu Talib called him back, and assured him that he would not be abandoned by his family. While, however, this protection saved him from open violence, it could not avail to protect his followers, some of whom were so hardly treated that they were advised by the Prophet to emigrate to Abyssinia, and at one period over 100 of them, mostly young men, had found protection there. Still he gained converts, and in the sixth year of the call he was joined by his uncle, Hamza, a man of wealth and influence, and by Omar, a warrior of great strength, strong will and resolute courage, whose influence on the Prophet and upon Islam was of the most marked character. Further, he gained converts outside Mecca, and though he nearly lost his life in an attempt to gain the people of Taif, he received the adhesion of the people of Yathreb, afterwards called Medina, who had been impressed by his teaching when on their pilgrimage to the Kaaba. In the midst of these labours he lost his wife Khadijah, and her death was soon afterwards followed by that of his uncle, Abu Talib, these events being followed by increasing hostility on the part of the Koraish. At last matters reached a crisis. A plot was formed for the assassination of the Prophet and the suppression of his party, so that early in 622 AD he commanded his followers to emigrate to Medina, and the same year followed them himself. It is said that the front of his house was watched by a number of men who had leagued together to join in his assassination, but that the Prophet, with Abu Bekr escaped by the back, while Ali lay upon the bed covered with the green rope of Mohammed, so as to deceive his would-be murderers. When the Koraish discovered the deception they respected the friendship which had dictated it, and permitted Ali to join Mohammed unmolested. For three days the Prophet and his companions lay hid in a cave in the neighbourhood and when the heat of the pursuit had subsided they resumed their journey and arrived safely at Medina. The whole of the Mohammedan world dates its chronology from this flight, or *Hegira* (Hedschra), the year 1 of the Mohammedan era being the 622nd year *Anno Domini,* and the fifty-third of the Prophet's life.

The people of Medina at this period were divided into two intensely hostile clans, whose feuds had been a constant source of disquiet;

but the arrival of Mohammed secured peace by the union of these parties in the common cause of Islam. Very soon the Prophet was placed in the position of supreme arbitrator in all matters of dispute, and by the wisdom of his decisions he greatly strengthened his hold upon the people. His short creed, 'There is no God but Allah, and Mohammed is his prophet', was readily accepted, and the duties of regular prayer and systematic almsgiving were enforced in a way that made open dissent very dangerous. All true believers were enjoined to regard each other as brethren and all tribal and blood relationships were to be laid aside in the interests of the common cause of Islam. Soon the neighbouring Arabs saw a new community formed in their midst, which they were compelled to regard with wonder, not unmixed with alarm. Nor was the alarm unfounded, for as soon as the Prophet had consolidated his power at Medina, he directed his followers to commence a holy war against idolaters, and in 623 he ordered them to attack and plunder a caravan of the Koraish on its way to Mecca during the sacred month of truce. A similar attempt, made later in the year, resulted in the Battle of Bedr, in which Mohammed gained a great victory over the people of Mecca. This enabled him to break up the power of the Jews at Medina, whom he had tried in vain to conciliate and who had manifested considerable hostility to his claims. Some of these were banished, with the confiscation of their property, and others were assassinated, so that the remainder were obliged to appeal to the clemency of the Prophet, and to desist from all open opposition. In the third year of the Hegira, the Moslems were defeated by the Meccans at the Battle of Ohod, in which Mohammed himself was wounded. In the fifth year he was unsuccessfully besieged in Medina, by an army made up of the united tribes of Koraish, Solaim, and Ghatafan, amounting to 10,000 men; and after this army had retired without effecting anything, he took vengeance on the Jews who had assisted them, and ordered all the men, 600 or 700 in number, to be beheaded in the marketplace, the women and children being sold into slavery. One woman, after being compelled to become a convert, the Prophet took to wife. The following year he made an attempt, at the head of 1500 men, to make a pilgrimage to Mecca, and though prevented by the Koraish, the latter offered to sign a truce for ten years, and permit him to come the next year unmolested if he would withdraw till then. Mohammed accepted the conditions, and after signing the treaty, led his followers back to Medina. By the terms of this agreement he was left free to send his missionaries everywhere and the number of his adherents increased daily.

It took Wilbur just two years to be received into the Moslem brotherhood and take an Arab name – Safir Samaha. He did the thing properly and ordered Martha to bring him robes of the purest linen which he wore with a *kafier* over his head and a dagger at his belt.

He enjoyed the life, riding out with Hassan in the morning followed by the Great Dane he had brought with him from America. The dog, completely devoted to his master, was called Wellington. Wilbur was devoted to Wellington, but Hassan, of course, had the Moslem hatred of dogs and although he did his best to conceal this, Wilbur sensed that Hassan hated the dog.

Martha, on the other hand, tolerated Wellington. 'It is the beast of my lord,' she would say. So Wellington was safe from being poisoned by Martha, and the other servants merely scowled when Wellington growled at them.

Wilbur decided in his third year, as he was now a Moslem, to make the Haj, the pilgrimage to Mecca that all good Moslems, who have the health and can afford it, are bound to make at least once in a lifetime. He did not take Martha and, of course, he had to leave Wellington behind, for Wellington would have perished very soon on such a journey. Wilbur loved the pilgrimage. It took a whole fortnight. He worshipped at the Kaaba. He circumambulated the holy monument seven times. He lived very frugally and simply with his special clothes for the Haj, fasting by day. When it was all over he returned and to his delight nothing had gone wrong at the fortress. Martha greeted him with the words: 'My Lord returns and his maiden sheds tears of happiness.' Hassan looked as pleased as his dignity would allow and said: 'Welcome back, Lord Haji,' indicating that his master would now bear this proud title, having made and returned from the pilgrimage to Mecca.

The murder did not come until Wilbur's seventh year as an adopted Arab and a Moslem convert. It arose out of a trifle. Hassan had laid out his prayer rug in the morning, then returned because he had forgotten his Koran. When he came back Wellington had fouled the prayer rug which had been laid out facing Mecca. Hassan, enraged, took an iron bar and killed Wellington with one tremendous blow. Wilbur heard the commotion and saw his dog dead, his brain bashed in and over him stood Hassan with his weapon. It was the month of Ramadan and tempers were frayed by the fast. In a blind range Wilbur hit Hassan and knocked him down. Hassan got up, drew his dagger and stabbed Wilbur through the heart. He lived less than ten minutes

Even in the Lebanon at this time the crime was a serious one and had to be seriously regarded by the authorities, who had no wish to have trouble with Washington. Hassan was arrested and chained with manacles and a heavy neck chain as well. He was brought before the Turkish governor for sentence.

'You admit you killed the foreigner?'

'I admit it, Sire.'

'Why?'

'His dog defiled my prayer rug, an insult to Allah. Then he hit me. I fell and, blind with rage, I struck at him with my dagger.'

The governor thought for some minutes, then said: 'You did this deed in a natural anger but it cannot be excused. You must be imprisoned with hard labour for three years. But for the circumstances you would have hanged. Go.'

Legal processes in the Lebanon at this time were swift and there was no appeal.

For my part I much regret that Wilbur Dangerfield died at the hands of Hassan his henchman because, had he lived, he might in his way have become as great and as formidable a character as Lady Hester Stanhope, the unforgettable Englishwoman.

9

An American Monster

When the Himalyan peasant meets the he-bear in his pride,
He shouts to scare the monster, who will often turn aside.
But the she-bear thus accosted rends the peasant tooth and nail.
For the female of the species is more deadly than the male.

When Nag the basking cobra hears the careless foot of man,
He will sometimes wriggle sideways and avoid it if he can.
But his mate makes no such motion where she camps beside the trail.
For the female of the species is more deadly than the male.

When the early Jesuit fathers preached to Hurons and Choctaws,
They prayed to be delivered from the vengeance of the squaws.
'Twas the women, not the warriors, turned those stark enthusiasts pale.
For the female of the species is more deadly than the male.

Man's timid heart is bursting with the things he must
not say,
For the Woman that God gave him isn't his to give
away.
But when hunter meets with husband, each confirms the
other's tale –
The female of the species is more deadly than the male.

Edwardian crime in America did not follow the English pattern. It was much more extrovert and brutal. There were, of course, the gang crimes in the city and these were directed by men. The outlaw and the highwayman had not yet disappeared from the American scene, while the syndicated gangster of the prohibition era was to emerge twenty years later when the Mafia took over the control of lucrative crime in America. Whereas crime in the thirties was largely controlled by foreign immigrants, during the third decade of the century crime in America was still an American product.

From 1900 to 1910 American crime was still centred outside the city. The gangs would roam the countryside and enter a town only to carry out their coups. Twenty years earlier they had still ridden on horseback as Jesse James did, but in the period we are discussing the railway provided the transport and at the very end of the period the motor-car was already starting to play its part.

American criminals at this time did not set their sights too high. They were content to rob a coach or, more rarely, to rob a bank. There were select criminals who specialized in the bank-robbing business. This was made much easier for them by the fact that nearly every town in America had its own small bank, usually run by the wealthier citizens of that place. This small bank often could not afford the elaborate security measures which the big bank adopted as a matter of routine. In fact it was not very difficult to rob a small bank. It was much more difficult to get right away without murder, and to dispose of the money without running into trouble.

Murder in America at this time was still a much more common occurrence than it was in England. England was small and had a fairly well-organized police force. Although each county had its own constabulary, it was controlled from London and criminals could be pursued from one county to another county without let or hindrance. In America each state still retained massive independent powers of investigation and the machinery for calling in federal aid was slow and cumbersome. The more experienced gangs found that they could flit around this vast country, starting from scratch when they entered a new state and made it their headquarters.

The murders of the period often arose from the fact that nearly every citizen had a gun to defend his property, and this is a tradition that still persists today. It is a legacy of the earlier times when the settlers were pushing the Indians further west and the Mexicans further south. America was still a very young country, turbulent and exciting, and the spatter of gunfire was a sound which every citizen had heard at one time or another, and which because it was so common did not cause much alarm or call for immediate action.

Rival farmers, if they had a serious dispute, would often shoot it out, not with the idea of killing anyone but to warn the other man off. The bank robbers were, of course, armed to the hilt, and if their escape was threatened they would certainly use their guns, which often resulted in a dying man being left biting the dust on the highway.

The great gold-rushes were very tough affairs, and in the atmosphere of the saloon where the prospectors gathered at night to drink brandy and rum, a shooting incident was almost part of the routine; and, finally, duelling lingered in the free atmosphere in America nearly a century after it had been stopped in Britain.

There was one special department of murder at this time in America that was unique and extraordinary. It was murder by women of their husbands or lovers in order to rob them of their money. Belle Starr had set the tradition thirty years earlier, but Belle was really an outlaw in a more classic mould. She used her beauty, her brain, her horsemanship and her ruthless courage to plunder the victims whom she ensnared. They were always men. Belle was not interested in other women and steered clear of them. Although all murders are horrible, Belle had a certain style and dash that made her into a folk legend. It was just possible to think of Belle Starr as a perverted heroine, because, although she was cruel and arrogant, and although she killed without compunction, she was also very feminine, with all that term implies.

I regret to say that the subject of this case, Mrs Bella Gunness, was entirely evil, except that she was apparently devoted to her children and the houses she occupied rang with the happy cries of children at play. However, these were not the only cries heard in the Gunness house, for Bella Gunness was a murderer on a scale never achieved by anyone before or since. It had been reckoned that during her life she committed nearly a hundred murders.

How could this matter happen? Let us consider the special circumstances that made it possible.

Bella Soresen, who later became known as Bella Gunness, was a Norwegian. Her first husband had died after giving her three fine children and then twice within three years Bella's house caught fire and was completely destroyed On the first occasion the insurance company paid out after only the usual formal enquiries, but on the second occasion they were very suspicious. Could it be that the woman was an arsonist? Or employed an arsonist? They paid only after long and exhaustive enquiries had revealed nothing at all. Bella was not a talkative woman. All she would say was, 'Know nothing. House burnt. Lost everything.'

As soon as she had collected – the second time – Bella decided it was time for her to move. And she knew exactly the kind of place she was looking for. At last, after some months' search, she found it.

In Indiana she found a rambling and fairly isolated small-holding where she could bring up her children and they would enjoy any amount of country air and roaming space. It was also ideally suited for other purposes she had in mind. Mr Gunness died of an axe wound. Mrs Gunness, with her children around her, attended the court investigation and told the jury that this heavy axe, very sharp, had apparently fallen from a shelf and killed the poor man. She completely captivated the all-man jury, who tendered her their condolences and deep sympathy. This is almost incredible, but it happened. Her story was so thin that one would have thought that even a jury of unsophisticated and susceptible Indiana farmers would not have been fooled.

Bella, of course, had a thumping insurance on her husband's life and, in view of the verdict of the jury, what could the company do but pay out? They did, however, know of her former successes in the insurance field and the company were determined that, whatever happened, innocent or guilty, they would never pay out to Bella again. The note they sent her made their message abundantly clear. Bella was no fool. She knew that the insurance racket was over. That if she ever claimed again – for anything – they would hunt her down for a kill. She never touched insurance after this, never paying a premium, and never, of course, making a claim. After all, she had done very well out of insurance companies. Two fires and a death, a small fortune which enabled her to buy La Porte, her conveniently removed smallholding.

Now that the insurance game was obviously played out Bella decided to open up a new line of business. Perhaps she could take the money off the men by direct action, having first tricked them, on some plausible excuse, into drawing a large sum in gold from the bank.

She inserted an advertisement in the local paper and it was a gem: 'Cultured, wealthy gentleman invited to get in touch with rich young widow of attractive appearance with a view to marriage.' The address followed.

She had any number of replies to choose from. Men far outnumbered women in Indiana at this time They were at a premium. And rich, attractive, young widow . . . . Oh, boy!

Bella proved herself an adept correspondent. After all, the man was now in the position of an applicant, almost a supplicant.

His curiosity was aroused. And, from Bella's point of view, she had already warned off the impoverished. So, if she asked for a very substantial deposit ' to ensure that we are engaged on a serious business ' the men could hardly refuse. They had implied that they were well-off by replying to Bella and a deposit, however substantial, as earnest money, was not altogether unreasonable. Besides, Bella in her letter said that it was her intention for her future husband ' to control all my affairs and receive all my fortune in his name '.

Fair enough, but there was the age-old defect in all this, namely, that Bella got the cash first and that the rest was only what the lawyers call ' promises *in futuro* '.

So Bella was really a con-woman as well. But she had, up to now, committed no offence, for promises *in futuro* cannot, either in American or English law, be made the basis of a charge of gaining money by a false pretence. Bella had baited her hook very cunningly. Male vanity was at stake and male greed may have been appealed to. It depended on the man. The first letters the aspirants wrote to Bella in answer to her advertisement told Bella a lot. She had now become an astute psychologist. She knew just what would make men behave in a certain way.

So she replied to each would-be husband differently, playing on the weaknesses that their letters had revealed. She had a very fine line of verbal allure:

> You, sir, are obviously a man of taste and discernment. Your educated, and indeed cultured letter tells me as much. I think I have been fortunate that you were moved to get in touch with me and when we meet I feel sure that we shall find we share the same ideals and pleasures when the day of our marriage arrives. But first you will want to meet me and see if I fulfil your expectations. We should not rush matters, for our whole future happiness depends on our mutual agreement and decision.

What common sense . . . . What delicacy of feeling. What a woman! And businesslike too. The whopping deposit did not put the gentlemen off. It made them all the keener. Here was no petty, bickering, nagging little housewife. Here was a woman who thought big . . . .

Now, at this point the story of Bella becomes somwhat sordid. For she carefully staggered the visits of her victims, who all went to La Porte never to return. Bella kept a fine sharp axe, her ' headsplitter ', and she would murder her victims in the night, burying them on her own land as opportunity arose.

It was crude. It was dreadful. But it was effective. Because of the nature of their assignation the victims had hardly ever informed their relatives of where they had gone to. They had just – vanished. They had joined the most anonymous fraternity in the world – that of the missing persons, mere names and numbers in dusty, discarded police files.

Bella was an exceptionally powerful woman and if her suitor was elderly or not robust she did not even have to use her lovely sharp axe. She would strangle the sleeping man, drugged with drink, with her own great peasant hands until he stopped his stertorous breathing and was very, very dead.

It was in 1908 that the brother of one of Bella's swains – Andrew Hoodgren – managed to trace his brother to La Porte. He became very suspicious indeed and organized a widesweeping hunt for his lost brother who was, in fact, peacefully buried at the end of Bella's charming old-fashioned garden – hollyhocks grew exceptionally well at the spot, shooting up to nearly twice their normal size.

Things were undoubtedly getting hot for Bella. And Bella always kept a jump ahead of events. They were never allowed to catch up and confront her. Out of the blue the rambling old-world house of La Porte was burnt to the ground. A farm hand, Roy Lamphere, was charged with arson, but the evidence against him was unsatisfactory and he was released after a short imprisonment.

Then the strangest event took place. Bella's garden was dug up. And the corpses were discovered. And in the burnt-out ruins of La Porte the bodies of a woman and three children.

Most writers on this extraordinary woman have concluded that Bella was dead. But was she? And, if so, how did it happen? Had Roy Lamphere, out of pique and revenge for some slight or injustice, really set fire to La Porte, causing the death of Bella and her family? Had Bella herself, learning that exposure was imminent, lighted her own funeral pyre in the manner of a Hindu widow before the abolition of Suttee? Or had she contrived to have another woman and other children burnt to death, making her own escape? I incline to the second theory. She had lived dangerously. Rather than face exposure she died dangerously by her own hand.

She left a portion of her considerable fortune to an orphanage. Bella had always been devoted to children.

10

Travel By Train?

I have always been fascinated by the background and structure of murder. Country-house murders in Edwardian days had a distinct flavour, mellow, sophisticated killings that took the house-party, but not always the servants, by surprise.

Murders in Edwardian Soho were certainly reported at the time in a characteristic way. At this time all Orientals were ' inscrutable '. The English, of course, were frank and fine, an open lot who told all they knew. This illusion pervaded the popular reporting of all Edwardian murders in which foreigners, especially Asiatics, were concerned. Chinese were the best copy for the journalists, but an Indian fakir or an African would do almost as well. They were all sinister, secretive, un-British.

Then the Edwardians dearly loved a good place name. If a girl had murdered her unfaithful lover in Forget-me-Not Lane, the press were home and dry. The name could be so innocent that it provided a pleasing contrast to the foulness of the deed – Cherry Blossom Common; or in itself sinister and forbidding – Hangman's Corner. These names would surely be splashed in the banner headlines of the popular press and chalked up by the pavement vendors of the press, who were much more numerous than they are now.

In fact, all street occupations were more busily pursued. Women wrapped in shawls sold flowers, usually in the form of a button-hole rose for the gentlemen. Shoe-blacks clustered round the railway-stations, and, of course, in London at night there were some thousands of women on the streets selling their bodies.

Motor-car murders were only just coming into their own.

Although the Sunbeams and the de Dion Boutons were, to say at least, erratic in their performances, the idea of using them as murder weapons to run people down deliberately had not been developed. Aeroplane murders – blowing up the whole plane by a planted bomb – were, of course, far in the future.

Murders in carriages and hansom cabs were not unknown but they were not convenient. There was always the difficulty of the driver, and even the horse might object and run amok if he sensed that there was murderous chaos going on behind him in the cab.

The seaside cliff – such as you still see unprotected at Brighton – was much in vogue. I suppose this was because it required only one determined shove and the deed was done. One could then rush for help saying that one's sweetheart had slipped and fallen over the edge of the cliff.

The locations for murder were innumerable and most murderers, naturally, sought privacy for their crimes. If no one saw the deed being done there would be no eye-witnesses and this might well save a murderer from the gallows. In order to secure privacy, assignations were made for meetings on a lonely moor, but then again it was difficult to arrange a meeting without leaving some kind of evidence of the invitation or its acceptance. The note which said, 'Meet me Saddleworth usual place 7,' might hang a man: so might a girl's casual words to her mother: 'I'm going out to meet George,' with her mother's reply: 'Don't be late.'

There was one place in which no arranged assignation might be necessary and that was a railway carriage on a train without a corridor, occupied by a man alone – the victim. The carriage was isolated, almost soundproof, secret, subject to the exact timing for arrival at stations, with only one link with the outer world – a communication cord.

Of course, one did not know in many cases whether the man one intended to rob and murder would ever take a train, and if one did know that he was going to do so, one did not necessarily know which train he would take and, most important of all, whether he would have a carriage alone.

But suppose that a man travelled by train once a week as a matter of routine, always catching the same train, always seeking a carriage that was unoccupied, always carrying a large sum in cash with him to pay wages after the train had reached its destination, then one was in a position to plan both a robbery and a murder. The murder was not the object of the operation. It was an essential sequel. The victim might struggle, and even if he meekly handed over the money bag he would raise the alarm as soon as he arrived. The police would be on to a very hot trail indeed, fortified by a good description of the robber, his clothes, height, manner of speech, facial characteristics and so on. And he might well bear scratches and bruises, not yet healed, on his body. Better then murder him and shove him under the seat, hoping that the corpse would not be discovered until the train returned to its depot, or station of origin, for cleaning. Even the most careless cleaning woman would probably manage to see a huddled man under a seat with possibly a trickle of blood on the floor. 'Gave me quite a turn, sir,' she would report to her supervisor.

These were the circumstances which existed for one of the most brutal of Edwardian murders, which at the same time presented the authorities and the public with an acute problem which the jury at the trial had to decide.

The facts of this terrible case were not really in dispute. It was the deductions that could properly be drawn from these circumstantial facts that were the subject of heated debate in the press, in court, and, more reticently, among those whose duty it was to see that justice was done.

It was early spring, 1910. Winter was still holding the north country firmly in its grip. Snow still lay on the Pennines and in Cumberland and on the Border. But work went on as usual in the collieries. Men had to work. The coal had to be mined. The men had to be paid. Their wages of four to five pounds a week seem paltry now. At the time they were the highest-paid manual workers in the country. Although individual wages were small the aggregate weekly wage for a colliery came to a substantial sum – three or four hundred pounds. The men lined up to receive their wages, cap in hand, and each man said: 'Thank you, sir,' to the manager who was paying them. They saw nothing odd in this. It was natural and only polite.

The men entrusted with the wages by the colliery owners – the mines, of course, were all in private hands – were very carefully chosen. They did not have to take any psychology tests or play with green and red balls, but the owners, through their managers, chose only men who had shown themselves naturally honest. They argued that a man was either honest or dishonest by nature. If he was honest, temptation would not even occur to him. He would say to himself: 'It isn't my money.' And that would be that.

In addition to natural honesty, they were looking for a man who had been with them for years, who was happily married and who did not drink. John Nisbet fulfilled all these requirements. He was perfectly happy with his job. He enjoyed it. He loved his wife and their two small girls. He was proud of his house which he had bought for £575 on a mortgage, and he looked forward to the ten days in September when the whole family went to Blackpool for their holidays. The men, of course, took their holiday earlier, but John Nisbet was a clerk and cashier, a white-collar worker, far removed in social status from the miners themselves. He was also a friendly little man and quite a good chess-player. On a winter's evening when his work was done one of his neighbours, who also played the game, would come in and, sitting near a log fire, the two men would play their game, arguing and teasing one another and enjoying every minute of it while Sarah Nisbet made tea for them.

John Nisbet was a daring, dashing, chess-player and so sometimes he was over-bold and met defeat. But he had his successes too. It seemed that some hidden, gay and adventurous spirit that never ventured in his business came out when he sat down with a chess-board and the chessmen who sprang to life as the game progressed.

It was a Friday. That was pay day, and it was 18 March and business was as usual. The head office had given John £380 to take to their Widdrington colliery to pay the staff and men. It was an hour's run by train from Newcastle.

There was a convenient train at 10.30 which would get John to Widdrington in time to pay out before the shifts came up for their ' dinner '. Sarah, as was her custom, came to the station with him. She liked to see him off. As the train was pulling out another man got into the carriage with John. Mrs Nisbet waved and the train shuffled off, blowing a great belch of steam as it went.

It was a stopping train and the porters would often look into the carriages and perhaps pick up some discarded newspapers or turn in any property such as umbrellas that might have been left behind. At Alnmouth a porter looked into the carriage that John Nisbet had taken. He noticed a trickle of blood on the floor. Then he saw a body huddled under a seat. He pulled it out, calling his guard. It was John Nisbet. He had been shot through the heart and eyes. There was no sign of any bag or any money.

The most intensive enquiries were made, for it was soon realized that robbery had been the motive for one of the most brutal murders of the century. Passengers were questioned and many of those who had travelled on the train volunteered evidence. As usual the large volume of evidence that the police gathered contained only some reliable and authentic nuggets of truth.

But there was enough. A man called John Alexander Dickman who, at one time, had been employed as a colliery cashier but had got into disfavour with his employers – who, of course, sacked him instantly – had been seen to get on to the train that John Nisbet had taken. Had he got into the same carriage? It was not certain. The Nisbets knew Dickman slightly, but Mrs Nisbet could not say if the man who had jumped into her husband's carriage at the last moment was Dickman or not. Or had he got into another carriage and then changed into John's carriage at the last moment?

The Police knew something about Dickman. He did not have a record but he was known to be without regular employment and was thought to be living by backing race-horses, surely the most disastrous way of attempting to earn a living that this generous world offers us. He was a surly, disagreeable man, except in drink, when he was all amiability and large ideas.

The bag was found without the money at the bottom of a disused pit shaft, not far from the station where some passengers said they had seen a man like Dickman getting off the train. Dickman was in dire financial straits at this time. He paid off one or two creditors after the murder, but said he had won money at a race meting that had, in fact, just taken place.

So here was a very difficult as well as a very horrible case. Dickman had the motive and the opportunity to commit this murder. But had he done it? No one positively identified him. He did not break down when questioned. He said he had been at home that day. His wife confirmed that he had been in the house all day. They had had a row, that is how it stuck in her memory.

Lord Coleridge was the presiding trial judge at Newcastle Assizes when the case of Rex *versus* Dickman came up for trial. Lord Coleridge was a judge of the old school. In private life he was a kindly and cultured man. On the Bench he was stern. He contrived, perhaps without realizing it, to surround the prisoner with an aura of gloom and guilt even before he pleaded the charge.

Tindal Atkinson prosecuted. He was one of those lean, somewhat cadaverous barristers who look at you through their spectacles and see a great deal. The prosecution in this case was more effective than the defence. Dickman was convicted of wilful murder with malice aforethought.

Lord Coleridge donned the black cap and passed sentence of death, making no comment other than the formal: 'May God have mercy on your soul'.

As the day for the hanging approached there was considerable public excitement and some outcry of protest. Dickman was known in his neighbourhood, yet no one had come forward to identify him. Even the wife of the murdered man had failed to do so. Dickman clung tenaciously to his story that he was absolutely innocent. Could a mistake have been made?

The answer must surely be that a mistake could have been made. Yet the thought of leaving unsolved this terrible crime which had bereaved a widow and her two daughters of the man they loved was more than the jury could bear. They found Dickman guilty, perhaps because there was no one else on whom society could take its revenge.

The case raised the whole difficult and dangerous question of the amount and strength of circumstantial evidence necessary to justify a conviction in an English court. It was one of those most difficult borderline cases. The jury believed, as I believe, that Dickman was the murderer, but perhaps my judgement is influenced by the fact that he was suspected, much earlier, of murdering Mrs Luard, again with a gun, again for valuables, and again in a lonely isolated place. Yet to believe a man guilty is not enough. It has to be proved and it was evident to the press and to the public that the evidence in the case was not conclusive. The chain not only had weak links, one or two links were missing. It was a case which in Scotland should have resulted in a reluctant verdict of 'Not Proven'. In England, both legally and logically, that should be interpreted as 'Not Guilty'. If that had been the verdict, as perhaps it should have been, I am sure a vicious murderer would have gone free.

This brings us to the real question of the reliability of trial by jury under judicial direction. How sure is it that verdicts are just?

Is trial by jury the best method of ensuring that the guilty are found guilty and that the innocent go free?

There are at least two alternatives to trial by jury. The first is to leave it all to the judge, whose whole training from his call to the Bar as a young man has been directed towards an ability to assess and weigh evidence, whose training as an advocate has, through years of experience, enabled him to differentiate between the nervousness of innocence and the nervousness of guilt. Why pay judges their high salaries and not make full use of them in deciding the one vital question that all criminal trials are held to answer: the guilt or innocence of the prisoners charged?

I think the answer to this is twofold. First, the jury system has its roots deep in the English way of life and in English law, going back at least to Magna Carta.

Glanville, the legal historian, tells us of the ancient roots of jury trial:

Though there are some traces of the trial by jury in the four reigns which immediately succeeded the Norman Conquest, it was not till a century afterwards, in the reign of Henry II, that this institution became fully established and was reduced to a regular system. The law of Henry II introduced the trial by assize or jury in real actions, as a mode of deciding facts which the subject might claim as a matter of right. In the reign of John we first begin to trace the use of juries for the trial of criminal accusations. It is quite clear, however, from Bracton and Fleta, that at the end of the thirteenth century the trial by jury in criminal cases had become usual, the form of the proceedings being given by them in detail. Introduced originally as a matter of favour and indulgence, it gained ground with advancing civilization, gradually superseding the more ancient and barbarous customs of battle, ordeal and wager of law, until at length it became, both in civil and criminal cases, the ordinary mode of determining facts for judicial purposes.

Until the end of the thirteenth century the only qualification required for petty or common juries, for the trial of issues in criminal or civil courts, was that they should be 'free and lawful men': *freemen*, as holding by free services or free burgesses in towns; and *lawful* men, that is, persons not outlawed, aliens, or minors, but entitled to the full privileges of the law of England. The statute 6 George IV. c50, entirely remodelled the law respecting juries. By this statute 'every man (with certain specified exceptions) between the ages of twenty-one years and sixty years, who has within the county in which he resides £10 a year in freehold lands or rents, or £20 a year in leaseholds for unexpired terms of at least twenty-one years, or who, being a householder, is rated to the poor-rate in Middlesex on a value of not less than £30, and in any other county of not less than £20, or who occupies a house containing not less than fifteen windows, is qualified and liable to serve on juries in the superior courts at Westminster and the courts of the counties palatine, for the trial of issues to be tried in the county where he resides, and also to serve on grand juries at the sessions of the peace, and on petty juries, for the trial of issues triable at such sessions in the county in which he resides '.

Nowadays all ratepayers who are of age can be called on for jury service. The limitation of age is now eighteen, but the limit of sixty remains. You can be Prime Minister at sixty, seventy or eighty, but not a juryman.

With roots as deep as this it would take a great upheaval to oust the jury and replace them by the judge. The English have always liked amateurs and distrusted professionals. And they have at least some reason for this. Certainly, in many fields, the professional debases what the amateur has tried to keep uncorrupted. Although, on the whole, judges are respected as doing a good job, there is no doubt that the public feel happier with the most vital question being decided by the concurrence of twelve men and women who may be more in touch with life as we live it today than the rather precious and protected persons that judges are apt to become.

Another alternative, of course, is to call in the scientists. Administer the ' truth ' drug. Consult the computer. This would face even stiffer opposition.

The so-called ' truth ' drugs vary in their effects from patient – if that is the right term – to patient. Used on some subjects they are accurate and very revealing. On others they are equally misleading. The thought of computerized justice is horrible to contemplate. Computers have already ruined ordinary business for the customer. One cannot any longer obtain a simple statement from a bank, one can no longer enquire how much one owes a computerized firm. Your computer number is the key to a great deal of private information gathered about you. Although computers rely entirely for their accuracy on the material fed into them, the results they give out are often regarded as holy writ. The further apart the administration of justice and computers are kept the better.

So we are back with our fallible jury system that may make mistakes but inspires more trust and confidence than any other method of attempting to arrive at the truth.

One overwhelming reason why we should not trust the judges with giving verdicts that may affect our liberty or even our lives is the inborn pedantry of lawyers. They are brought up in a blinkered world where they are taught coolly to assess the 'facts'. But facts are sometimes fictions and a jury of men and women will often have common sense that overrides the judicial view. All of us who have been in court in famous trials, both criminal and civil, have watched as juries, little by little, formulated their own view with the judge struggling to get them to adopt an entirely different interpretation of the facts. It is this independence of juries that is the most valuable single asset in the whole jury system.

A good many train murderers have not been brought to justice and there is no doubt that the single compartments of the old railway carriages without a convenient corridor helped the murderers greatly. However, train murderers have been caught, charged and hanged from time to time in the last century. The very earliest trains, of course, with their open carriages, did not give the would-be murderer a chance.

In 1880 a young writer, Percy Mapleton, murdered a man called Gold on the train from Victoria to Brighton. He murdered for money and was hanged. He was a very bad young writer, and he was not much better at murder, making a hopeless mess of the whole affair.

I travel between Brighton and London at least once a week and I can guarantee that on the Brighton Belle there is today no real scope for murder. The pullman coaches offer no privacy, the meals, including the breakfasts (with the worst kippers in the world), make each carriage a place of continual movement and chatter. Percy Mapleton would now have to resort to that old favourite the white high cliffs with their sheer drop to death, and even then everything, it seems, is seen by somebody.

There is something especially horrifying about the train murders. The victim is unlikely to be alarmed by the fact that he has a fellow passenger who can, making some excuse, get near him and shoot him or cut his throat. But there is that split second when the man about to die sees in a flash that his end is coming. It is the moment of sheer agony and terror.

Moreover, with murderers one never knows. Safe in the carriage with their victim they may be tempted to play with their mouse. There is some evidence that Dickman did this, revelling in the death-fear that he saw in John Nisbet's eyes. This horrible perversion, sadism run mad, is by no means uncommon and it occurred again quite recently when in the 'Moors Murders' a little girl was slowly tortured and done to death by the man and woman who had her in their power. It seems incredible that such people can actually exist and perhaps look much like everyone else as one passes them in a crowd.

If the evil mind of the murderer is distorted by perverted sexuality there is no deed that he will not do to gratify and assuage his passion, and this may be a motive no less strong than his greed for money.

These people may not be mad in the legal sense, but they are Satan's children and their unpredictable ferocity and bestiality cannot be measured by the standards of ordinary men.

II

Murder of the Police

The murder of unarmed police constables by armed criminals has always been treated as murder of the most heinous kind. It is not decreasing today. Since the suspension of the death penalty the temptation to a cornered criminal to shoot his way out to freedom is, at times, irresistible. He sees perhaps one man only standing between him and freedom, the man in the blue uniform. He realizes that for burglary with previous convictions he is going to receive a sentence of from seven to ten years. For murder the sentence may be fifteen years, reduced to twelve for good conduct. The awful sanction of the rope is no longer there. The criminal fires, the policeman falls – dead; and for a time at least the murderer goes free.

It is this very situation that is the strongest argument for retaining the death penalty for all murder, for when the death penalty exists in England the criminals do not carry guns. It just is not worth while. They calculate the advantages and disadvantages shrewdly enough and their decision is: 'If we might hang for it, no guns ....'

In August 1966 we had the most recent and, in some ways, the most awful example of criminals murdering police to escape detection and arrest. It happened in Braybrook Street, Shepherd's Bush.

Detective Sergeant Head, Detective David Wombwell and Constable Roger Fox were on patrol in a police 'Q' car. They were in the district because a rumour had reached them on the underworld grapevine that there was going to be an attempt to 'spring' Frank Fraser, a gangster held in nearby Wormwood Scrubs Prison.

The police spotted a Standard Vanguard and recognized one of the men in it. They flagged the car to a halt, but the Vanguard, its engine still running, dodged and drove off at speed. The police car was fitted with a special engine and eventually overtook the Vanguard. Detective Wombwell strolled over to the Vanguard to take particulars. As he was about to speak to the driver he was shot through the heart. He died on the road. Sergeant Head sprang to the aid of his comrade and was shot through the eyes. Then the most ghastly and cowardly part of the affair took place. One of the gangmen walked over to the 'Q' car and shot the constable who was driving. Constable Fox died within thirty seconds. The Vanguard drove off at high speed. Dying, Constable Fox scribbled the number of the gangster's car on a scrap of paper and threw it into the rear seat of the 'Q' car.

There had been no crime of this enormity since Police Constable Gutteridge thirty years earlier had both eyes shot out while making an enquiry of a motorist. And the Braybrook Street crime was the more terrible and deliberate of the two murders.

The police were not going to allow their comrades to be slaughtered in this way without getting the criminals and at last they did so, arresting the gang responsible. But nothing could bring the three young policemen back to life, nothing could assuage the grief of their families. The names of the three heroic policemen appeared in a Roll of Honour published next day. In the entrance hall of New Scotland Yard on the wall is inscribed a more permanent tribute and memorial. It reads:

Police Sergeant, 2nd Class (CID)
CHRISTOPHER TIPPETT HEAD
Police Constable
GEOFFREY ROGER FOX
Temporary Police Constable (CID)
DAVID STANLEY BERTRAM WOMBWELL

On 12th August, 1966, the three officers when on duty in a 'Q' car, stopped a suspect car containing three men in Braybrook Street, Shepherd's Bush.

While PS Head and PC Wombwell were interrogating the occupants, two of them left the car and produced firearms. PC Wombwell was shot at short range. PS Head was shot alongside the police car. The three officers were killed within the space of a few seconds.

In Edwardian days, before the First World War, horror of this scale would still have been thought of as impossible. The criminal fraternity – the villains – were still a closely-knit community. They did not murder, for they knew that if they did they would be hanged. The Home Secretary at this time advised the Queen to remit a death sentence only in cases where an injustice was suspected or on compassionate grounds, as in the case of a mother who, made unstable by childbirth, had suffocated her child.

It was only when amateurs entered the field that there was danger, because amateurs did not know the rules. They had no code, no ' understanding ' with the police. They might carry loaded firearms, and they were more apt to bungle the job they were on and be discovered and so in danger of arrest.

Such a case was the murder of Inspector Arthur Walls by John Williams. The case had several unusual features, and in the behaviour at the trial, in the characteristic police methods adopted, and in the sentence and its execution one sees the tough Tory mentality of the Edwardian era: an era which had absolutely no sympathy with murderers and thought them better dead.

Does the name Sztaray mean anything to you? Probably not. Yet if you had been moving in Edwardian society you would have known immediately that this was the name of a great, noble Hungarian family who had for centuries owned vast estates in that country and had supplied many ministers at court. The Edwardian era was a time when in London and in New York one could still know ' everyone '. Everyone, that is, in the small, exclusive yet immensely powerful world of the rich and the privileged.

Countess Flora Sztaray lived at 6 South Cliff Avenue, Eastbourne. She had bought the house on the death of her husband, a wealthy Hungarian nobleman. When the countess settled in England the London press reported her arrival and made a feature of her fabulous jewels, which included a diamond necklace said to have been presented to her on her birthday by the Emperor Franz Joseph. Her collection of diamonds, sapphires, rubies and opals was indeed beautiful and very valuable. Yet the countess insisted on keeping her jewels with her wherever she went. She refused to deposit them in her bank, saying that there was no point in having beautiful jewellery and hiding it away. The press also reported this remark and quoted the countess as saying: 'I have reached an age when I need a little embellishment.'

No doubt more than one member of the criminal fraternity had read these items with interest, but it was unfortunate that John Williams should have been included in the number. John Williams had several names which he used, and he was in the habit of saying that he was an American born in New York. As far as we know this was quite untrue. He was thirty years of age.

On an October evening the countess had ordered a cab to take herself and her cousin to the Burlington Hotel, where they were to dine with some friends. As soon as the cab drove off the driver turned to the countess and said: 'I thought I saw a man crouching behind the doorway of your house.' The countess looked at herself in a hand mirror which she carried and realized that many of her most valuable jewels were still locked up in a drawer in her bedroom. She told the driver to turn back and immediately telephoned the police. Impressed by the importance of the caller, the police sent Inspector Arthur Walls to investigate. The countess and the inspector both thought that the man, if he had not gone away, would be upstairs in the bedroom searching for the drawer that contained the jewellery and forcing any drawer he found locked. In this they were completely correct. The intruder was upstairs in the bedroom busy with his task. Inspector Walls shouted to him to come down. The reply was a series of shots, the first of which killed the policeman.

The robber, who had now become a murderer, made good his escape. The police were left with very few clues. They had the bullet which had entered the inspector's heart and from this they knew the type of weapon which most probably had been used. But nobody had seen the man in the bedroom or, at least, they had not seen his features. He had shown agility and speed in escaping from the house, so presumably he was a young man. It was not a great deal of information upon which to found a murder hunt.

In the story of crime culprits are often caught through their wives or the women with whom they are associating. John Williams was living with a beautiful young woman, Florence Seymour, at 4 Tideswell Road. Florence was pregnant and expecting a baby of whom John Williams was the father. However she had other admirers, one of whom was a most unpleasant character, Edgar Power, who had been trained as a doctor but had failed his exams. He was now a petty criminal. Edgar Power bitterly resented the fact that Florence had turned him down to live with John Williams and he decided to take his revenge. Power knew that the murderer and would-be burglar was Williams, who had summoned Power to help him after the murder. He had seen Williams going to bury the revolver and some rope in the sand.

Edgar Power went to the police to betray his friend.

The police who, of course, were determined to get their man, decided to use Power in order to frighten Florence Seymour into taking them to the place where the revolver was buried. As soon as Florence and Power reached the spot a number of police who had been waiting came forward and arrested Florence, and Power as well, but they released Power the next day, keeping Florence Seymour in custody. The police then threatened Florence, saying that unless she told the whole story she, herself, would be charged with murder because she had helped John Williams to conceal the crime. The conduct of the police throughout the entire investigation showed fairly clearly that they were prepared to stoop to any methods which would give them the evidence which they needed to convict Williams.

John Williams had retreated to London where he hoped to hide himself until the police pursuit of the matter became less hot. It is possible that this would have presented great difficulty to them. Fortunately they had the services of Edgar Power, who again was willing to play the role of Judas. Power sent a message which he knew very well would reach Williams, telling him that he wished to give him a letter from Florence. They should meet at Moorgate tube station. The trusting Williams turned up and Power greeted him. This was the sign for the police to appear and arrest Williams.

John Williams was the son of a north-country clergyman. He was an educated man, well dressed and well spoken. He denied that he had anything to do with the murder. At this stage one cannot help considering the possibility that Edgar Power had been more involved in the matter than he cared to admit. However, the police now had sufficient evidence. They had the evidence of Florence. They had the evidence of the recovered revolver and they had the evidence, for what it was worth, of Edgar Power. And, of course, they had John Williams in custody.

At the court proceedings Williams wore a veil which partly hid his features and the newspapers described him as the 'Hooded Man'. It was never explained why the prisoner should have been veiled but one cannot rule out the possibility that he had been the victim of brutality while he was in police custody. There was no doubt that the local police bitterly resented the murder of their inspector, and this was natural.

The first proceedings took place at the police court in Eastbourne. The most important witness was Florence Seymour. She was very soon to give birth to her child and the court had much difficulty in obtaining her evidence, for she now realized she had been tricked into giving an account of the affair that might hang her lover. At this stage Williams was not represented either by a barrister or by a solicitor but, at the suggestion of the court, a young Eastbourne solicitor agreed to act for him; this young man instructed Patrick Hastings, who was then active in the south-eastern circuits, and was later to become a famous advocate and law officer.

When Hastings first read his brief he fastened at once on to the question of intent. Suppose that in view of Florence's evidence the jury would not believe any kind of alibi, if they were assured that in fact John Williams had fired the shots, one of which killed the inspector, still had those shots been fired with intent to kill or merely to scare off anyone who attempted to come upstairs towards the bedroom? It seems quite possible that in fact this is what happened. It is assuming a great deal to suppose that Williams, the amateur, interrupted on the job, crept over to the balustrade and, taking careful aim, shot the policeman dead. It was at least as likely that the shots, fired in panic and at random down the stairs, were intended to facilitate the robber's escape.

But even so it might be murder, for there is a doctrine in English law of 'constructive' malice and intent. This being translated out of legal jargon means that if I am engaged on one crime – robbery – and, albeit accidentally, commit another perhaps more serious crime – murder or manslaughter – my intent carried over from the first crime to the second, for the law holds those who engage in criminal activities liable for all their acts that arise out of those activities, intended or otherwise.

A harsh doctrine? Perhaps, but it has a kind of basic common sense and even validity about it, which is more than you can say of many judicial and legal doctrines.

As Hastings continued to study his brief, his mind working along these lines, he saw at once that a plea of 'Guilty' to manslaughter might conceivably be accepted by the Crown. But here he came up against the resolute refusal of the prisoner, who said: 'Nothing doing. I am innocent of the murder and I plead Not Guilty. I've been in prison before and I'd rather hang than go back ....'

In the face of this there was nothing that Hastings could do except to fight the case for an outright acquittal. The judge would put the case to the jury as one of premeditated murder and point out that the lesser offence of manslaughter had not even been pleaded. We may well ask whether a man's life should in any way be determined by legal pleadings. Should not the judge be expressly empowered to review the whole case apart from the plea that the prisoner insists on making, quite apart from the way in which he answers the charge? Personally I feel the judge should always be responsible for putting before the jury alternative courses that they may take in returning their verdict, alternatives that, though they may not have appeared in the prisoner's plea nor in the speeches of his counsel, nor in cross-examination, have, nevertheless, emerged during the trial. It is good to have exact rules of procedure and determination of 'issues'. It is even better that the system should be flexible enough to enable the jury's verdict to achieve justice. For this, not procedural matters, must always be the one ultimate aim of all criminal trials.

This famous trial came on for hearing at the Court House at Lewes just before Christmas. It caused immense excitement not only locally but in the national press as well. It had all the ingredients of high Edwardian drama.

First of all John Williams was, apparently, a gentleman-burglar, so the press could present him as a kind of Raffles. This was no mere factory worker who had bludgeoned his wife to death. This was an educated and well brought up young man who had turned to crime and so found himself in this terrible predicament. The Edwardian public was always truly shocked when a 'gentleman' got into serious trouble.

Then there was his mistress, Florence Seymour. She was beautiful with a strange, ethereal loveliness and she was pregnant by her lover. She had been duped twice and bullied and badgered by the police. She had much public sympathy.

Edgar Power was a revolting little rat. He had pretended all along that he was helping Florence when, in fact, he was revenging himself on her because she preferred John Williams to himself.

The public was also avid for news as to how far the police had actually gone to get their man. They did not like the fact that Williams was always hooded. Had his face been smashed in by the infuriated police?

Then, for good measure, there was this fabulous foreign countess who evoked brilliant and colourful pictures of the glamorous court of the Austrian Emperor and his galaxy of arch-dukes with their high-born wives and glittering mistresses, perhaps the most romantic court in Europe with the Emperor arriving late at a great ball to the strains of that most nostalgic of all anthems, the old imperial anthem of the Austrian Empire.

Down in the quaint little assize town of Lewes, this really shook them. One of the Sussex newspapers in a moment of understandable over-statement declared: 'Lewes is now the centre of the Empire.'

When the trial and the assize opened and the judges made their progress from their lodgings to the old court, the very narrow High Street was packed with spectators, including some of the local gentry who had come into town to see the show. The trumpeters heralded the arrival of the judges in their scarlet and ermine robes and this was the climax, for half-an-hour earlier there had been intense excitement as the 'hooded' prisoner arrived – handcuffed to two police constables. The witnesses too were instantly recognized: poor pregnant Florence; Edgar Power, betrayer of his friends; and the countess herself, who drove over from Eastbourne in a carriage and pair and looked the part of an Austrian aristocrat to perfection.

Sir Frederick Low, who led for the prosecution, asked for leave to put Florence Seymour in the box first as she was soon to give birth to her baby.

As Florence now said that her evidence at the police court had been given because the police constantly threatened to prosecute her for murder, counsel for the Crown was allowed to treat her as a 'hostile witness', and she was so severely cross-examined by the legal 'gentlemen' that she collapsed in the witness box. However she was briskly revived and the cross-examination continued. Eventually, apparently on the point of having a miscarriage, she was led weeping from the court.

Edgar Power had a gruelling time in the witness box and it was clear that he was a pathological liar. Hastings had no difficulty in showing this witness up for the unmitigated blackguard he was. If the Crown had had to rely on him alone, John Williams must have been acquitted. But there was other evidence: the revolver – its finding: a hat found near the scene of the crime – Williams' hat, the prosecution said. At least it fitted him. Then this fitted in with Florence's story that John Williams – whom she referred to pathetically throughout the proceedings as 'my husband' – had left the house briefly on the night in question to return hatless. At the moment that Power entered the witness box and was taking the oath John Williams half rose from his seat in the dock as if to make towards the man who had betrayed both him and his mistress. The warders closed round him and the incident passed, but it made an impression on all who saw it.

The judge, Mr Justice Channell, pointed out that it was quite possible that the man who fired the shot intended it to be a warning shot and not a shot to kill Inspector Walls. Then he instructed the jury on the doctrine of constructive murder in the terms I have already explained.

The judge had clearly come to the conclusion that Williams was guilty and should be convicted. He dealt at great length with the revolver, the circumstances of its findings, the fact that it had been cleaned by the prisoner – to remove fingerprints? – and the fact that the revolver used in the killings was, according to the experts, of the same type.

I always regard this type of evidence as being especially unreliable. For instance, a man is stabbed in a London street with a knife which a witness describes as 'a butcher's knife' and a butcher's knife is found cleaned in the home of the accused. The assumption that the knives are identical is most dangerous. There may well be fifty thousand butcher's knives of similar design in the metropolitan area, most of them cleaned after use . . . .

The jury took their cue from the judge and found John Williams guilty of murder with malice aforethought. The judge, who appeared to be unmoved by the tension that had affected many people in court, passed sentence of death and the trial ended in banner headlines in the evening papers.

Of course there was an appeal. Patrick Hastings, a first-rate lawyer and appeal court man, argued the case for the prisoner. The long and closely reasoned argument really had three basic points on which it relied:

1 No one had seen John Williams fire the shot and no one had identified him as being anywhere near the scene of the crime.

2 The judge himself had admitted that it was quite possible that the shot that had been fired was not intended to kill Inspector Walls.

3 Hastings argued persuasively that the jury should not have been told, as in effect they were, to compare the evidence which Florence gave in the first proceedings in the magistrate's court with that given by her on oath at the trial. For the first story had been told under a terrible threat, that of a murder charge, and the evidence had been virtually dictated to her by the police.

It was all to no avail. Lord Alverstone, the Lord Chief Justice, one of the least distinguished lawyers to hold that great position, took the attitude; 'The man's guilty, and that's all there is to it.' There had, he said, been no miscarriage of justice.

But the Appeal Court is there to consider whether the prisoner has been rightly convicted on the evidence and that is a different question to the court's own assessment of his innocence or guilt.

Without calling on counsel for the Crown, Lord Alverstone dismissed the appeal. Never was a man's life dealt with more speedily or in a more summary manner.

Even now the drama was not over.

A man called 'Freddy Mike', who had been referred to by Williams in his evidence as the man who had given him the rope, asking him to get rid of it, wrote from Brixton Prison saying that he had evidence of vital importance to reveal that would upset the verdict against Williams. The solicitor, accompanied by an Inspector Burrows, visited Freddy Mike who told them that the murder had not been committed by Williams at all, but by a continental burglar who had escaped to the continent. He gave a certain amount of corroborative evidence to support his story.

The public, of course, heard through the press of this new development and the Home Secretary was closely questioned about it in the House of Commons. Mr Reginald McKenna, the Home Secretary, stoutly defended the judicial decision both in the Court of First Instance and in the Appeal Court. He said he found that there was no real substance in the story of Freddy Mike.

The Home Secretary made a long and careful statement on the case in the House, as indeed he had to, for questions had been put to him by both the great parties and even by members of the new 'Labour' party. Some of his logic sounds a little strange:

> The House will understand that there is no part of the Home Secretary's duty which puts greater responsibility upon him or is indeed more painful, than that which has to be exercised in connection with the prerogative of mercy. Of course, any man would be only too glad to find a scintilla of evidence or reason, or I might say to invent a reason, which would enable him to save a human life. But my duty, as I understand it, is to act in accordance with the law and the traditions of my office.

The only reason for interfering with the course of the law, he went on, was if there had been any subsequent evidence brought forward which would justify reconsideration of the case.

He then proceeded to deal with the letter from Freddy Mike.

> I have investigated that story to its very foundation. I have traced the family history of the man who calls himself Freddy Mike, and I find beyond question, and I may say even on his own admission, that there is not a shred or shadow of foundation for his story from beginning to end. He said that he had a twin brother. He had no twin brother. He said that the twin brother or a friend of the twin brother was in Eastbourne that night. There were no such people, and the whole story is a pure invention, as he himself now admits, written and concocted by him after reading the evidence in a newspaper, and because, having known John Williams in the past, he did not like to think of his being hanged.

When the Home Secretary came to deal with the ticklish question of 'constructive' intent he did so in these words.

> If one looks at the question from the other point of view, and considers the fate of the unfortunate policeman, one whose example is followed in scores of cases year by year – and they carry their lives in their hands, themselves unarmed with pistols, and never hesitate

to arrest a burglar whom they find at his trade – and if a burglar who shoots and kills in these circumstances is not to be held guilty of murder, we should be doing a grave injustice to the police.

This was an outright reaffirmation of the doctrine that a burglar who accidentally shoots someone while he is feloniously occupied is in law a murderer.

What did it all add up to? The trials, the legal arguments, the summing-up, the verdict, the appeal, the final result. I think what it all amounted to was an implacable determination on the part of the authorities to protect the unarmed police. And can we say, if this is openly admitted, that they were not justified?

In Edwardian times, as now, public order and security, the freedom of the ordinary member of the public, the integrity and very sovereignty of the nation, depended, in the last resort, on the ability of the police to apprehend the law-breaker.

In King Edward's day the Establishment, backed by the public, acknowledged this basic fact and they were fully prepared to crush the burglar or the murderer if they could catch him.

And yet these rare and not very well organized criminals were no real threat to the general public, as are the organized political gangsters of our day, the Black Power fanatics, the Trotskyists, the followers of the mad Mao Tse-Tung, the whole rabble of manipulated protest aimed at overthrowing all the liberties we have won. These people are a real and dangerous threat and it seems that the Establishment is far less resolute in dealing with them than our fathers were with a much smaller menace.

The politics of England during the seventies are going to be in great part the politics of direct action, of organized violence in the streets, the traditional forum of revolution. In battles in the streets violence will increase until we have murder in the street and savagery falling short of murder. We can take a lesson from the firmness that our fathers showed, restore the rope and the birch and be prepared to use against the thugs the violence they do not hesitate to use against the public and the police. There would be squeals of horrified protest from the fellow-travellers in Parliament, but very quickly it would be made clear that for young and old alike, for rich and for poor, there is but one law and those who wantonly defy it will meet with the resolute severity of the courts.

A few hangings and a few floggings and the whole evil conspiracy that is aimed at English life and freedom as we know it would collapse.

I hope it is not left too late.

12

The Law Errs

There is a peculiar system in England whereby the legal profession is divided into barristers-at-law and solicitors. The former are governed by the Bar Council and the latter by the Law Society. Solicitors only may be approached by lay clients – you and me – and these clients can contact their barrister only in the physical presence of their solicitor, who 'instructs' the barrister in a document, appropriately bound in red tape, called the 'brief'.

This odd system results in a pleasing duplication of fees and in much lucrative muddle which the poor litigant or prisoner has to pay for unless he is state-aided.

I mention this historical situation and the race of Brahmin lawyers we call barristers, because in 1921 I was such a young barrister at 3 St James's Square, Manchester, where the cotton comes from. We had our Bar mess in the Midland Hotel, Manchester, which, at that time, was a very good hotel indeed. It was my job as 'junior' of the circuit to travel round at assize time with the circuit butler and the circuit silver and to preside at Bar mess. The other towns and cities on the northern circuit were Liverpool, Lancaster, Appleby and Carlisle.

The Bar mess was upstairs on the first floor and when dinner was over the younger barristers were wont to make their way to the 'French' restaurant which sometimes had a cabaret and where, in any case, the more likely looking girls in the north country were apt to be seen in the evening.

On our way to this Mecca we prudently visited the gentlemen's lavatory so that we could remain outwardly sober and serene throughout the evening. One night at about eleven o'clock I had made this wise pilgrimage when the attendant said: 'Do you know who that was, sir?' I looked round and saw a stocky, grey-haired man vanishing through the swing door.

'No. Who was it?'

'Oscar Slater. Reckon he was lucky.'

Then I knew just who the man was, for Oscar Slater had been convicted of the murder of Marion Gilchrist in the High Court of Justiciary in Edinburgh nearly twenty years before and had only just been pardoned and awarded £6,000 as *ex gratia* compensation. I suppose we might say that this sum represents about £25,000 today. It was not much for two decades of wrongful imprisonment, but then the Scottish establishment and the British Home Office have always been extremely careful to abide by two principles in cases – which rarely arise – where they really have to pay something. The first principle is to pay as little as possible, which means the award of a sum just large enough to prevent a concerted public outcry; and the second guiding rule is to delay payment as long as possible. I hasten to add that these principles are accepted and religiously pursued by all Government departments and are by no means the exclusive preserve either of the Home Office or of the Scottish Judicial authorities.

The Oscar Slater case aroused enormous interest because it was a case in which the Scottish police and prosecuting authorities, as well as the Scottish Bench, had blundered from the start, blundered, as it were, with their eyes open, implacably determined, it seemed, to kill their hare though it was the wrong scent, and quite possibly the wrong hare.

English lawyers, of course, could take a detached and not uncritical interest in the matter, because when Scotland took over England she naturally retained her own legal system and her own special criminal procedure. It differed in many important respects from that which has been evolved over the centuries in England. I have not seen it pointed out – though no doubt some commentator has made the point – that, by and large, the English system appears to be motivated by a determination that, so far as is humanly possible, no innocent man shall be convicted of a crime he did not do, while the Scottish system appears to be actuated by an equal determination that on no account shall a guilty man escape. The English system appears to be founded on certain sporting considerations bound up, in some mystical, feudal way, with the code of the English gentleman, while the Scottish system appears to be very conscious of the mission of the law as an avenging angel.

This difference in motivation and approach is, of course, reflected most strongly in the dual verdict in Scotland of 'Not Guilty' and 'Not Proven'. Meaning roughly: 'He did not do it' or 'We cannot prove he did it.' In England both these verdicts are, in fact, combined in the verdict of 'Not Guilty' which lets the prisoner go free whether he is absolutely innocent or whether the prosecution has failed to prove their case beyond all reasonable doubt. The English, bless their generous hearts, thought it unfair that any stigma that might attach to the verdict 'Not Proven' should attach to a man not convicted of any crime, and I think they were right. We should never be misled by the spurious assumptions of the scientific approach. Law is made for men, not machines.

Occasionally in this book, but rarely, I have asked the reader to indulge in gentle mental exercise in order to understand the background of a particular case. This is necessary in the case of Oscar Slater, for not only was it a murder charge in the hands of the Scottish police, it was also a case in which that very Scottish official, the Lord Advocate, prosecuted and the final verdict was arrived at by a distinguished Scottish Bench and jury. For this reason I ask you to digest this description of the differences between the Scottish and English legal systems, as they were fifty years ago, taken from a contemporary case in which these distinctions were at issue:

In Scotland the prosecution of criminal offences is entrusted to public authority. For this purpose the kingdom is divided into districts in each of which there is a procurator-fiscal charged with the duty of investigating and prosecuting all offences occurring within his district. In this he is aided by all the local authorities, such as sheriffs, magistrates, police. The whole of this machinery is under the control and direction of the lord-advocate, assisted by the solicitor-general and four or five members of the bar termed 'depute-advocates'. Private prosecutions are not indeed incompetent, yet so well does the above system work that they are practically unknown. For the same reason perhaps the office of coroner has become obsolete for more than two hundred years. The grand-jury was always unknown to the law of Scotland; though since the Union it is summoned, when cases of treason are prosecuted, in the English form of 'oyer and terminer'.

The distinctions of felony and misdemeanour are unknown; but grave offences involving capital punishment or penal servitude are appropriated to the High Court of Justiciary or its judges on circuit, while minor offences may be prosecuted before inferior courts, whose powers of sentence do not exceed two years imprisonment. Several offences, no longer capital in England, still remain so in Scotland; but the public prosecutor always restricts them to an arbitrary punishment.

When an accused person is arrested, he must without delay be brought before a magistrate, in presence of whom he makes what statement he chooses, and who may remand or commit for trial much the same as in England, with this difference, that the procedure in Scotland is secret. In all charges not capital the accused is entitled to bail; in capital offences he can only be bailed with consent of the lord-advocate. The Habeas Corpus Act does not extend to Scotland, but in lieu thereof is the Act of 1701 c. 6, in virtue of which a prisoner may compel the prosecutor to bring him to trial and have the trial concluded within 100 days, with the alternative of his being for ever freed of the charge. Fifteen days before trial the accused must be served with an indictment containing a list of the jurors and of the prosecutor's witnesses, and of such articles or documents as will be produced at the trial. On the other hand, the accused must lodge in reasonable time a list of such witnesses as he intends to adduce. As a rule no other evidence is admissible on either side than that above mentioned, nor can any one serve on the jury whose name does not appear in the above list. In all cases the accused is entitled to legal aid in the preparation and conduct of his defence. If he is unable to procure this, it will be furnished by the court. If the charge is found relevant a jury of fifteen – not twelve, as in England, is balloted from the list above mentioned, both prosecutor and accused being allowed certain challenges. The prosecutor then leads his proof, followed by that for the defence. Both parties may then address the jury, but so that the accused shall have the last word. After the judge's charge the jury consider their verdict, which may be in one of three forms: Guilty, Not Guilty, or Not Proven. They are not required to be unanimous; a verdict by a bare majority in any of the above forms is sufficient. The legal effect of *Not Guilty* or *Not Proven* is the same – viz. that the accused is acquitted and can in no circumstances be again tried on the same charge. When a verdict of guilty is pronounced the prosecutor may or may not move for sentence. When he does so the judge discharges his function; if he declines to move for sentence, which is sometimes the case, the judge is powerless, and the prisoner must be dismissed from the bar. And here it is to be observed that there is no such thing in Scotland as a new trial in criminal cases after the jury have delivered their verdict. If a guilty man escapes, whether on a verdict of not guilty or not proven, or because the prosecutor declines to move for sentence, he is for ever discharged. If an innocent man is convicted by a miscarriage of justice, the only remedy is a royal pardon, unless where the High Court quashes the proceedings on a matter of form. There is no appeal to the House of Lords. Police offences and cases of a trifling kind are tried under certain statutory forms without a jury. But the general principles above mentioned are carried out.

These peculiarities in Scottish criminal law – viz., the tying down of the prosecution to the list of witnesses, the verdict by a majority, and the finality of trials – have often been commented on as inimical to the interests of justice. And certainly, if applied to a system based on private prosecution, they might produce dangerous consequences. But associated as they are in Scotland with a public prosecutor who has no interests but the ends of justice, who will not prosecute without reasonable grounds, who has the most powerful and elaborate means for discovering the actual facts, and who will at any time, if he see cause, drop the prosecution, they have not been found to work otherwise than beneficially. It has been claimed for the Scottish criminal courts that they have an inherent power of punishing acts which are *mala in se*, though not declared crimes by the legislature. And such a power has justly been characterized as dangerous and unconstitutional. It is doubtful, however, whether in an absolute sense it ever existed. In Scotland, as in other countries not possessed of a code, certain acts have always been punished as crimes, though the statutes making them such are no longer extant; and well-known

> crimes do not lose that character because their mode of perpetration has, with a change of manner, become somewhat varied. Bearing this in mind, it will probably be found that the Scottish courts are to the full as careful as the English to abide within the limits of the British constitution

Maybe. But the British constitution does not exist in any written form, large parts of it at this time were mystical ' prerogative ' and, in any case, the Scottish courts were very proud and independent and were not at all worried whether their findings fitted into the format of a ' British ' constitution. Nor were they prepared to depart one iota from the criminal and police and court procedures that were part of the Scottish system. It just happens that in the case of Oscar Slater, owing perhaps mainly to the police obduracy reinforced by special pleading by the supposedly impartial Lord Advocate, and finally given the accolade of a verdict by the jury on the direction of the Bench, justice slipped up, came a terrifying cropper and lay there bruised and humiliated on the legal pavement.

These were the simple facts.

Miss Marion Gilchrist was a wealthy old Scottish lady of eighty-four. She lived in a most comfortable flat at 15 Queens Terrace, Glasgow. On 20 December 1908 she sent her maid, Helen Lambie, out to buy an evening paper – the old lady liked to keep up with the hectic events of the day, the social gossip, the international news and the appalling crimes that the poor always seemed to be committing.

When the maid returned, a Mr Adams who lived in the ground floor flat said: 'Hurry upstairs. I heard a great commotion coming from your mistress's apartment.'

As Helen entered the room a man brushed past her and tore down the stairs. Poor Miss Gilchrist lay prostrate, battered to death, her head smashed in by blow after blow from some blunt but lethal weapon. A young girl, Mary Barrowman, was nearly knocked down on the pavement outside No. 15 by a man running from the building. The police wanted that man. Neither the maid, Helen Lambie, nor the girl, nor Mr Adams, in spite of police prompting and suggestion, could really describe the man and, in any case, their descriptions were quite different. It was obvious that they had not seen his features nor accurately noted what he was wearing. The police, after they arrested Slater, tried to improve on this, but the most the two young women would say was that Slater 'was like the man' they had seen tearing from the building. This basic weakness should have warned the police to be careful, but then they had what appeared to be a stroke of luck. A small trader in the city told them that a man called Slater had been trying to sell a brooch, crescent-shaped, in the clubs of Glasgow. Thieves tried to dispose of their robberies in this way to avoid the records kept by the pawnshops, many of whom were well in with the police.

Now only one piece of jewellery was missing from Miss Gilchrist's collection – a brooch – and it was crescent-shaped. Then the police discovered that the brooch had been offered for sale before the murder – and that it was not Miss Gilchrist's brooch anyway. But they decided to press on. The arrest of Slater took place in America, for Slater had travelled there with his mistress after the murder. But he was extradited and put on trial and the whole ramshackle case against him was supported and strengthened by Mr Alexander Ure, KC, the Lord Advocate, who told the jury that Slater was an evil man 'capable of committing this crime'. No doubt this was true in part, but it was not the issue the jury should have been trying. It was not the issue which the judge should have directed them upon. Their verdict should have been determined solely by whether, according to the evidence, Slater had committed this brutal murder, not whether, by nature and inclination, he could have done so.

What was it that made it possible for the authorities to hound Slater when they must have known that their evidence against him was far from conclusive? Well, first of all, he was a Jew. His real name was Lecchziner. Now I do not suggest for a moment that the Scottish establishment in good King Edward's day was anti-Semitic. Nor do I think that the Jews as a race invariably endear themselves to their Christian neighbours in the host country in which they choose to settle. But it is absolutely disgraceful if it can be shown that racial prejudice can, in any way, influence criminal proceedings. Mind you, at this time nearly everyone in England had racial prejudice – and was proud of it. It was so palpably clear that the English were the chosen race of the modern world, that anyone who suggested that Indians, Africans, Italians, Arabs or Jews should be regarded as equals was looked upon as soft and eccentric, not to be taken seriously.

I do not doubt that if the police, finding their evidence so insecure, had been prosecuting a God-fearing Scotsman of good family, the case would have been dropped.

But Slater was not only a Polish Jew, he was a rogue. He did not work. He lived off gambling and the immoral earnings of women. He was an outrageous and stinking offence in the nostrils of the puritanical Scottish establishment. Here was this human reptile who had defiled the fair name of Glasgow and who had now fled with his whore to America to escape the long arm of the law of Scotland. When they got him back, the authorities had no intention whatever of letting him go. The police were convinced they had got their man. True, no weapon had been found, no bloodstains had been discovered to connect Slater with the crime, but here was this curious incident of the brooch. Perhaps the witnesses had got their dates wrong? But the witnesses would not budge. Anyway, why had Slater 'fled'? Slater said he had made preparations to emigrate months before – a likely story. Or even if he had, might he not have committed this awful crime knowing he was soon to quit the country?

I do not blame the police too much for being captured by their own convictions, but when we come to the Lord Advocate it is a very different matter. He should have put the evidence before the jury with absolute impartiality. He should have noted both its strength and its weakness. He did not do so. He too seems to have been captured by the spirit of the chase. The summing-up was careful and cautious but quietly damning and the verdict was a majority verdict. We do not know how the fifteen jurors were divided. We shall never know, but, at the time, rumour had it that it was only the odd vote that went against Slater.

The police took enormous trouble with the case. Mr Adams, Helen Lambie and the girl Barrowman were all sent to New York to identify Slater in the extradition proceedings. In the clear cool air of winter in New York they seemed to be much more resolute and certain than they had been at home in identifying Slater as the killer and the New York court did not hesitate to declare that a *prima facie* case had been made out, and that Slater should be returned to stand his trial in Scotland. But when the three key witnesses had to face the awful responsibility of their evidence in the Supreme Court in Edinburgh, they were much less sure and fell back on their original statements that the man had charged out of the house like a madman and all they could swear was that he had been quite like Slater, a big man with a burly appearance, powerful but very active.

This was a description that would obviously fit some thousands of Glasgow citizens and many members of the underworld that has always lived precariously in the teeming slums and sleazy clubs of that city.

When the judge passed the sentence of death, Slater sprang up and said: 'I know nothing about this. You are convicting an innocent man.' But 27 May was fixed for his execution.

However the Home Secretary advised the Queen to exercise her prerogative of mercy and Slater was sentenced to life imprisonment. That, it seemed, was to be the end of the Oscar Slater story. Not so.

Writers are often a nuisance when they poke their noses – as they are apt to do – into matters outside the realm that they have made their own. But on the whole they are in Britain a fearless breed, and again, in a general way, they hate injustice. Conan Doyle led a bevy of distinguished writers – authors and journalists – who pointed out that the evidence in the Oscar Slater case fell far short of that proof 'beyond all reasonable doubt' that the law demands.

At first, of course, authority was deaf, but slowly, as the din of protest increased, the Government could not but hear and it was decided that the file on the Oscar Slater case should be given a new and searching look. There was, of course, a new Home Secretary and that helped too, for, if a mistake had been made, then obviously no one now in power, either in the judiciary, the police or the home office, was responsible. It is much easier to correct other people's mistakes than it is to admit one's own.

Then, at last, the public woke up to the fact that a man had languished in prison for nearly twenty years convicted on evidence that was far from conclusive. The public joined the writers in protest and at last the subdued protest became a roar. Oscar Slater was released and grudgingly awarded his £6,000, compensation at the rate of about £1 per day for twenty years of wrongful imprisonment – not excessive. If our lords and masters were as careful of our cash in other fields we would have little cause for complaint.

The Oscar Slater case is by no means unique and we should, I think, consider whether such miscarriages of justice could be perpetrated today and if they could, can anything immediate and effective be done about it?

Apart from the figures that suggest that the number of outright miscarriages of justice are rare, there is some evidence that, in fact, a number of courts of first instance, including magistrates' courts, do make fairly regular mistakes. If there is an appeal all may be well. If, as often happens, there is no appeal, the wrong decision, involving perhaps unjust suffering, stands.

The coroner's court is a fertile and frequent source of bad decisions. It is thought that twenty-five per cent of deaths through murder slip by this court as 'death from natural causes'. If this is even approximately correct it is a horrifying figure.

The man charged with a major crime, if he has money, can hire the best talent in the country to defend him. But if he has no funds? He will be allotted a solicitor and nearly always a young and inexperienced counsel. Excellent for training the young lawyer concerned, but hard on his lay client.

It is surely utterly wrong that the conviction or acquittal of a man, on which his liberty for life may depend, should vary according to his purse. The situation is inexcusable and the only remedy is the massive law reform supported by both political parties at election time but then speedily forgotten, or, if not forgotten, handed to the lawyers themselves for implementation – which comes to the same thing.

The public, it seems, could not care less. Only when the rare sensational case, such as that of Oscar Slater, hits the headlines does it raise curious eyebrows and speculate whether all is well with the law. But such matters quickly pass. Almost any story for the newspapers is better than law reform, which reeks of musty books and pedantic practitioners living lives far away from Coronation Street.

The whole question of law reform is gigantic in its scope and includes a simple but comprehensive legal code for civil and criminal law that any layman can read and understand, the merging of the two branches of the legal profession to cut out divided work and fee duplication, and a National Law Service on the lines of the National Health Service, thus doing away with the great advantages which the rich now enjoy at law, and the corresponding disadvantages of the 'poor'.

Apart from these urgently needed reforms, which the lawyers themselves will not introduce in a hundred years – the vultures know when the pickings are good – there is the question of the miscarriage of justice to be tackled. It is a difficult question, but perhaps these reforms would go some way towards lessening the evil of unjust or mistaken decisions:

1 Abolish private fees, the system under which 'fashionable' silks are paid large sums by wealthy clients, thus obtaining a very special chance in any litigation or prosecution.

2 When appointing magistrates attempt to include a lawyer, preferably a retired resident, in the panel that constitutes the Bench.

3 Allow judges a week's grace in which to reflect on their

judgements and change them if, on calm consideration, they think they need alteration. This might cut out some expensive appellate work.

4 Confine judicial comment to the facts of the case and forbid general remarks aimed at discrediting or endorsing the witnesses who have been called and given evidence on oath.

5 Institute a nation-wide 'Don't go to Law' campaign, coupled with a 'Crime does not pay' campaign. Crime *is* a mug's game. Let the message get across. Forbid television to make heroes of criminals and drug-takers.

6 Increase the penalties for perjury. Perjury is one of the most serious crimes in the calendar and should be treated as such.

7 Let the judges every three years take a refresher course in factory or office, doing the work that ordinary pepole do and seeing the life ordinary people see. At present they are cocooned.

8 Let the prerogative of mercy or pardon be exercised by three committee men, with the Home Secretary taking the chair as the third member, and with decisions by a majority vote. The whole area of pardon is old royal prerogative country, and, as we cannot have the Queen making her own personal decisions in such matters – which might be by far the best solution – let's modernize the procedure, distributing the responsibility. As the Home Secretary cannot help being a political animal, his two co-adjudicators would be chosen from the world outside politics.

I do not pretend that the acceptance of any or even of all these proposals would make the law fair overnight, nor immediately do away with the occasional case of grievous error, but at least the suggestions should be debated. They would bring a breath of fresh air into the fetid and fusty atmosphere of the courts and the Temple.

If we do nothing now. If we close our eyes to law reform in all its major aspects, if we allow the lawyers to make a charade of reform by introducing piddling little 'reforms' that do not affect in any way the law as the public see it, and know it, and suffer from it, then some day, perhaps quite soon, ruder hands than ours will smash much that is good and fine and fair in English law, as they bring the law within the preconceived dictates of a one-party system and a police state.

The Summing-Up

We have been looking at vintage murders that took place in the Edwardian era, the short decade that was, in Britain, dominated by Edward VII, and his court, by the great beauties of the time – Lily Langtry, Mrs Cornwallis-West and others, and by the heroes of the literary and stage world, Sir Henry Irving, Ellen Terry, Sir Frank Benson and Charles Hawtrey.

Punch of the period reflects faithfully the accepted attitudes of the day. The upper classes were made the subject of appreciative laughter, but the lower classes were nearly always presented as slightly ridiculous. In the political cartoons Britain – the Bull Dog – was always right, resolute, and, in the end, triumphant, tearing the pants off unscrupulous Russians, ambitious and jealous Germans, and wild and woolly Americans and other colonials.

All this may seem childish, but it was not. This was a society still controlled by the King, the Lords and the Commons; and the big landowners in the country and in London wielded enormous influence. The dukes were a race apart, their London houses palaces. They attended the state opening of Parliament in gilded coaches drawn by matched carriage horses with coachmen and outriders. Society was quite small. You could not crash in with money alone. If you were very rich and behaved with decorum, taking a part in the life of the county as a lord lieutenant, a high sheriff or a justice of the peace, if you supported your local hunt, if you loved horses, especially race-horses, then, gently, slowly, and without any signal the doors would open – just enough to let you in.

It was a magic world you were invited to enter. A weekend

at Longleat or at Chatsworth was an experience. The family and twenty or so guests (that might even include the Prince of Wales) were waited upon by at least an equal number of retainers who, in the servant's hall, reproduced, in meticulous detail, the precedence and the protocol of the dining-hall for the household.

The world of England was the oyster of the great families. If, by ill-chance, a member, however remote, of one of these families lost his money, well there were always the colonies, or the Indian Empire. That the few should have and retain this kind of life was regarded still as natural, perhaps inevitable. The Labour Party and the radicalism of Lloyd George were still to come as revolutionary social forces.

Royalty regarded themselves as a race apart. This applied to all monarchs. King Chulalongkorn of Siam writing to Queen Victoria, after an appropriate and official opening, addresses his 'sister' – 'by reason of our regality'.

The Edwardian era was the last decade of absolute security for the old and wealthy families of Britain. The situation was never revived. Although the First World War was followed by a period of hectic gaiety in London, the thirties loomed ahead and the great houses were being sold off one by one. Families who had owned whole villages found themselves reduced to living in a single manor house with two servants and perhaps one hunter in the stables. A new England was emerging in which the workers, because they were so much more numerous, had decisive political power. The story of the manipulation of this new *imperium* by the former lords of life is a fascinating tale of adaptability and shrewdness.

For those who were not eldest sons, and so would not inherit estates, there were the professions. These were the Royal Navy, the Army, the Church and the Bar. No others. The professions of today, the solicitors, the accountants, the publishers, the dentists, the businessmen, these came later. Parliament, of course, was almost a closed shop and the House of Commons really had some claim to being one of the world's most entertaining clubs.

Because this was the structure, the dominant upper class was strongly represented in the law, and the judges in particular were drawn almost exclusively from those members of the Bar with a certain social background. If you were very clever indeed, a Rufus Isaacs or an F. E. Smith, then nothing could hold you back and, in the end, the Establishment absorbed you as Marquess of Reading or Earl of Birkenhead. Because the caste system in England had no rules, like the Indian caste system, it was stronger. You could not break it. It was not there to break. There were no untouchables. There were merely people you did not ask to dinner.

This social structure and background had a definite bearing on the law, lawyers, the courts, prisoners, crime and prison. It was a many-sided influence.

Because the judges were Establishment figures educated in the old public schools and the two universities, they had a reverence for authority as such and they had a healthy detestation for everything and everyone who threatened that authority. Criminals, of course, were the most obvious and overt threat.

The amount of real money involved in Edwardian crime did not really matter to a country as immensely wealthy as England was at this time. It was the outrage that the judges felt they had to deal with by massive punishment.

The punishment could take several forms:

It could take the form of penal servitude, and that meant the life of a hardworking slave without hope.

It could take the form of the cat-of-nine-tails, a process of lashing which literally tore the man's back to pieces.

For young offenders there was always the birch, a lesson they never forgot.

For the murderer, if he was sane, there was the rope. If he was insane, there was Broadmoor for life.

These were much the same punishments that were used in Tsarist Russia and still are used in the Soviet Union today, the only difference being that as a weapon against rebellious intellectuals – writers in particular – the Soviet Union has now resorted to imprisoning sane rebels in madhouses, a refinement of torture used hitherto only by the Chinese.

The judges never doubted for a moment that they were right,

that it was their bounden duty to terrify those brought before them and to join in the cross-examination if they sensed that the prisoner was slipping out of the net. Fortunately juries remained remarkably independent considering the pressures brought upon them.

The psychology and thinking of the Establishment approved of heavy punishment on grounds which today we have largely discarded, possibly to our peril. They believed in long sentences so that the prisoner at least could not repeat his crime for many years. They did not really believe in reformation. They believed in the efficacy of fear.

Their strong sense of property made them pass sentences that today would be regarded as monstrous but, in fact, we follow the same tradition today, regarding property as more important than life. The sentences on the train robbers is an obvious example. Nevertheless we do not send young people to prison for petty theft unless constantly repeated.

The judges certainly believed that the public enjoyed and were entitled to be gratified by the punishment of those who had broken the law. Vengeance, properly controlled and exercised, on behalf of the public by the Bench, was regarded as right and proper. Did not the Bible sanction it? It was a part of life, a human reaction, society's protest.

It followed, too, from all this that the Establishment of the judicature and the Bar was not much interested in penal reform. Prisons, they thought, should be places of horror and sadness and, my God, they were.

As for law reform that, of course, was entirely the concern of those who understood the mystique and the mysteries of the law, the lawyers themselves. The lawyers had no intention of reforming the law, or the cost of litigation, or the professional structure of the fraternity or indeed anything at all. Why reform a golden egg? They might tinker from time to time with new procedures but, basically, the whole judicial system would be left exactly as it had been for so long. Basically this system in 1971 is as it was in 1911.

The Edwardian attitude was reflected in Britain overseas.

The Prince of Wales writing to his mother, the Empress, from India, deplores the arrogance with which British officials treated even high-caste Indians. He was sure that this was wrong: 'They will be much more likely to be our friends and support us if we treat them with civility.'

The British had it deeply embedded in their mythology at this time that all dagos and all natives were untrustworthy. You did, of course, come across rare exceptions, but by and large Indians were shifty, lazy and inveterate liars. Africans, of course, were regarded as sub-human or only human in the most primitive form – 'just off the trees'.

Although these attitudes and their results may astound us today they seemed perfectly natural at the time. The word 'racialism' was not used. Everyone knew that the white men were superior to the brown men and the yellow men and, of course, all were superior to the black men of Africa and India. If one had asked them why they entertained these ideas they would have laughed or smiled tolerantly and replied: 'Of course they are. Anyone who has had to deal with these people knows that it is so.'

And the Edwardian Establishment had one convincing answer to all criticism – success. After all, here we were, a small island off the coast of Europe, the undisputed masters of a quarter of the globe, ruling a gigantic empire the like of which the world had never seen. To criticize the Establishment that had brought about this tremendous triumph seemed churlish in the extreme.

The Church, too, was a powerful force backing the Establishment, but at least it was candid about it. One felt that Christ had become an English gentleman. He had certainly lost his original race and nationality. So the courts carried on under the banner of God as well – 'And may the Lord have mercy upon your soul.'

The whole grand and glorious conception will offend most people today. I find it irresistible. I think this was the apex of the British story, a time when the rulers had convictions and were sure of themselves. Life was hard for the workers, but it was certainly gayer than life today. They may have been the servants of their masters, but they were not the enfranchized slaves of a socialist bureaucracy. There was still fun and adventure and opportunity to be had – and the clever boys grasped their chances. They were encouraged to claw their way up. They were not battened under the hatches.

The King was important to England as Head of State and vital to the law which was carried out in his name – Rex *versus* the Prisoner, King's Counsel, and so on. Fortunately King Edward VII was an outstanding man, not clever but very experienced and able. Most of the correspondence he had with his ministers is now available for reading and one cannot read it without realizing that his advice was constantly shrewd, directed not to details but to those major considerations of policy that protected the well-being of his country. His Home Secretaries already had the power of remitting the death sentence for murder at their discretion, but such cases were approved by the monarch himself. Now this is no longer the case. He was the last English king to take a direct part in the government of the country. After him the prerogative powers very quickly disappeared.

What are we to say of the vintage murderers whose exploits and crimes in Edwardian times we have traced in this book?

I think there is one vital difference that distinguishes them from murderers today. The Edwardian murderers were, on the whole, domestic killers motivated by passion, greed, a yearning for freedom, love or some allied reason. Today the typical murderer is the man who kills a police constable to escape arrest. This is a sinister change and the one real reason for reintroducing the death penalty.

There is no doubt at all that when the death penalty is there as a grim and awful warning, criminals do not – by an almost unanimous agreement – carry guns. They fear that if they did they might use them. Without the death penalty they carry guns and, in the last resort, use them. Why not? We are going to get twelve years for robbery anyway and the murder sentence will come to about the same with remission. And with the gun we may never be caught.

The police and the public realize this but Parliament, pathetically ' fashionable ', is carried along on a permissive tide, ready to listen to any arguments that may make it appear that the death penalty for murder does not deter

Tell that to a murdered policeman's widow.

I hope that it has been of interest to you to meet some vintage Edwardian murderers. Some were cold and calculating and altogether evil, but others were pathetic, the victims of their own natures or dire circumstances. They compare favourably, I feel, with the deliberate killers of today. The Kray brothers had no counterpart in the Edwardian killers' age. The day of the dedicated gangster was far in the future.

As you may have suspected, I look back to the Edwardian period with some nostalgic regret. It must have been a wonderful world – at the top.